Majoring in Motherhood

a crash course in Gospel truth for the hardest, messiest, most glorious job in the world

Emily Schuch

To my husband, who has been my constant encourager
To my dad, who taught me the power of words
And to my mom, the ultimate Mom Lady

CruciformPress.com | info@CruciformPress.com

"I've never met Emily, but she is now my mom-friend. She gets me. She knows the beautiful, messy chaos of raising children and, even better, she knows how to encourage my weary heart. You will consider her a friend too after reading her sweet book. She will make you laugh and think hard about why God has called you to major in motherhood. Best of all, she will point you to Jesus."

Kristen Wetherell, mom of three and author of *Humble Moms* and the *For the Bible Tells Me So* board book series

"*Majoring in Motherhood* is a joy-filled book that helps you to laugh at some of the truly trying days of motherhood with young children. Emily reminds us not only of the difficult task we undertake as moms but also of the deep significance and meaning of what is often seen as mundane and unimportant by our surrounding culture. We need to be reminded of the holy calling of motherhood and how God works in and through us as we serve our children. If you need encouragement as a mom of little ones, get this book and let Emily guide you into deeper thinking on our role as mothers."

Erin Kunkle, co-host of the Maven Truth Parent Podcast, mom of five

"Emily Schuch is the professor of parenthood you've been waiting for. In her masterclass on being a mom she shares a window into her own motherhood journey, the good and the bad, as she gives readers a crash course on leading a household and more importantly, how it teaches us the gospel of Jesus Christ. ***Majoring in Motherhood* is as witty as it is helpful and it'll bless any mom who picks it up.**"

Adam and Chelsea Griffin, parents of three sons, host the Family Discipleship Podcast. Adam is an author and Lead Pastor of Eastside Community Church

"***Majoring in Motherhood* will have you laughing and crying in the same chapter**, as Emily relates her motherhood experiences. Every mom can relate to her stories of motherhood, and will be encouraged by the Truth she shares. Motherhood can be one of the loneliest, hardest jobs in the world, but Emily reminds you that you are doing a holy, God-honoring work. **This is a great read for moms of any season**, but I can't wait to give it to new, expectant moms to read during those middle of the night feedings when moments of encouragement and laughter are hard to find."

Jenny Worsham, Co-founder of Gather Moms

"Emily did **an excellent job of communicating the hilarious, hard, beautiful, sanctifying, and relatable facets of motherhood while continually pointing back to the gospel.** The reminders of God's sovereignty, faithfulness, sustenance, and grace are both convicting and encouraging in ways that pushed me toward Christlikeness in motherhood. **This book ministered to me in more ways than I can count!**

Kristen Young, Social Influencer and Mom of 5

"*Majoring in Motherhood* is **an invitation to belonging for all mothers, reminding us we are not alone.** With relatable humor and treasures of biblical truths, Emily Schuch offers profound encouragement, inspiring mothers to live like Jesus. These parable-esque stories will strengthen those who are in the middle of the Hardest, Messiest, Most Glorious Job in the World."

Heather Jonsson, Bible Teacher, Host of the Bold Mercies Podcast

"**Spunky, hilarious, and oh-so-real. Schuch had me laughing 'til I cried.** With wisdom and wit, she created the world's first degree taught in a way that makes you feel like you're having coffee with a friend. That's my kind of major! Now, I finally know what I want to be when I grow up: a mom doing life alongside Jesus and ladies like Emily Schuch."

Kelsey Gillespy, author of *In the Trenches: Finding God Through Parenting Littles*

Majoring in Motherhood: A Crash Course in Gospel Truth for the Hardest, Messiest, Most Glorious Job in the World

Print / PDF ISBN: 978-1-949253-48-1
ePub ISBN: 978-1-949253-50-4
Mobipocket ISBN: 978-1-949253-49-8

Published by Cruciform Press, Minneapolis, Minnesota.

Contents

Orientation Day

Speaking One Mom to Another

I get the last load of laundry running while the other two finished laundry piles lie in a towering mound on my bed, waiting to be folded and put away. I tell myself that I am definitely getting to them today just like I told myself yesterday . . . and the day before. The laundry reminds me of the mythological Hydra—once you cut off one head, two more would grow in its place. Or in my house, once you get one load of laundry put away, two more appear in its place. At least that's how it feels sometimes—never-ending. *This is how I'm going to go*, I think. *The laundry is going to kill me. There will be headlines: "Local Mom Found Buried under Pile of Dirty Onesies."*

Once I close the washing machine lid, I move on to clean up the dishes and remnants of lunch. The dried applesauce that my son dropped under the high chair yesterday stares me in the face. *That's going to require hands-and-knees scrubbing. Don't have time for that.*

My applesauce thoughts are punctuated by the

call—not of the wild, but of the poopy and incompetent. "Mooooommmmy! I need you to wipe my butt!"

I successfully wipe the butt, then rush to change the sheets the baby leaked on the night before. Naptime glimmers like a beacon of hope. *You can do this. Just change one more diaper, sing "Jesus Loves Me" as fast as you can, and then you can go eat Ghirardelli dark chocolate as a reward ... quietly, so the "others" won't hear you.*

I get the baby down and close the door. *Victory!* But as I stand there in the corner of my kitchen, chewing on my chocolate prize, I start to wonder ... *How did I end up like this? The resident butt-wiper? Was this the vision I'd had for life?* I had potential once. I was going places. I'm not sure where those places *were* exactly, but I don't think they looked anything like the dark recesses of my son's closet that I planned to reorganize over the weekend. And I'm pretty sure they didn't include battling the Laundry Hydra or getting regular requests for butt-wiping.

I think back to the pictures of myself at my college graduation and laugh, maybe a little cynically. There I was, smiling with my diploma like the whole world lay at my feet, when what was really going to lay at my feet were my children while I tried to go to the bathroom.

College definitely seems like another lifetime. My world as a stay-at-home mother of four in Texas is drastically different than it was then. My roommates are a lot cuter but also a lot more likely to pee on the floor. Late nights are a thing of the past unless they involve someone wanting to use me as a pillow or a milk buffet. Sometimes, when I'm on my hands and knees scrubbing that dried applesauce off the floor or cleaning greasy handprints off my cabinets, I think to myself, *Wow, I'm so glad I got that philosophy degree. Plato's theory of forms is* really *coming in handy right now.* Or, *I'm sure glad I memorized over 200 reaction mechanisms in organic chemistry. I wish I could figure out the reaction mechanisms of my toddler.*

Whereas I once spent hours considering things like Thomas Aquinas' argument for the existence of God or the age-old debate of Calvinism vs. Arminianism, my brain is now mostly cluttered with the correct Tylenol dosage for a twenty-pound infant and an assortment of *Daniel Tiger* lyrics. I used to have an abundance of time to write and do pretty much whatever I wanted, and now, I'm lucky if I get a few minutes just to sit down and breathe.

It's not like motherhood was some kind of surprise detour. I'd always wanted to have kids. It was always part of the plan. But I don't know that I was totally prepared for the ways kids would change everything about my life. When I was a newlywed with zero children, I remember talking to a mom of six kids. She told me about how she was excited to get to go away to a conference. "Honestly," she said, "I just want to sleep the whole time." She definitely seemed dead on her feet. She looked a little dazed. I felt naïve compassion and wondered ... *is it really that hard?*

The answer was yes. Yes, it is that hard, but I don't know if I could truly have understood that then. I'm not sure anything could have *fully* prepared me for being a mom, but I do wonder sometimes if I could have been at least a little more prepared. While my education doesn't always seem very relevant to being a mom, I don't think it was a waste, and I have even found many parallels between the things I learned in school and the everyday life of motherhood. These overlaps have even led me to wonder, *What would a degree in motherhood look like? What should new, young moms know about the journey they've just begun and what on earth, if anything, does it have to do with Hume's theory of causality that I pored over my junior year of college?* This book is the answer to these questions. It's an entry-level course to get you ready for the hardest, messiest, most glorious job in the world.

Motherhood has stretched me and pushed me in so many ways. Currently, I'm seven years in, far from any kind of expertise or offers of a professorship, though I do feel like I have learned a few things. Motherhood has taught me so much about myself and about God. In this book, I have collected some of those lessons. I've tried to give you big doses of Jesus along with some humor because—let's be honest—some days, the only thing that can help us tread the fine line between sanity and insanity is a good laugh at the regular absurdities of life with small children. I've tried to make it fairly short and, hopefully, sweet because I know you hardly have time to read it, just like I hardly had time to write it. Maybe we can't call it a motherhood degree, but perhaps a kind of crash course—one that will at least get you through your final exams.

So, class. Let's begin.

1

Math

Exponential Laundry, Divided Sleep, Multiplied Love

When I was growing up, my mother, a former math teacher, emphatically told me that I was not allowed to hate math. I may have grumbled and complained through my nightly times tables worksheets, but I suppose I never actually hated it.

Later on, I somehow married a math nerd/statistics genius. His actual job is to use math and data to catch credit-card fraudsters. He fancies himself a detective … a very nerdy detective. Needless to say, I am sure he will be telling our children the same thing that my mom told me. And I am sure that I will never hear the end of it from either of them if I don't include mathematics in our motherhood crash course. So, this is for them: let's begin with math.

I studied math all the way through calculus, even solving for the resultant volume found when rotating a bounded area about the x-axis, but most of that knowledge has been replaced by baby sign language that I use for four weeks with each kid before quitting. I may only remember the basics of math, but I do remember enough to know that there are certainly some parallels between math and motherhood that might help us make sense of our daily lives as mothers.

Correlation, Variables, and Formulas

To my husband's shame, I never took a class in statistics, but he has explained one of its foundational concepts to me: correlation, or the relationship between things. One of the main goals of statistics is to use data to discover correlations in order to answer questions. For example, what correlation is there between age and the way people vote? What demographic of people is most likely to respond to ads for certain products? Or, what is the correlation between my listening to my husband talking about math and my head exploding? Because there definitely is one.

In motherhood, correlation is very important. Some things have positive correlations and others have negative correlations. Most of these correlations center around sleep. Did baby sleep all night? If yes, baby is happy and Mommy is happy: positive correlation.

But if baby woke up and refused to go back to sleep, baby is grumpy and Mommy is grumpy. My husband tells me this is actually still a positive correlation, but to me, it definitely feels negative.

I remember the first time my newborn son slept

for five consecutive hours overnight. Once upon a time, a mere five hours of sleep would have left me exhausted, but after a month with a newborn, I felt like a new person. I felt like I could conquer the world ... or at least clean the toilet. Maybe even get real jazzy and put on some mascara. Sleep is a major factor in the correlations of motherhood.

As you move past the newborn stage, though, things become a little more complex. If you can stretch your shrunken mom brain to hearken back to the days of algebra, you will remember that it was all about variables—factors that could alter the outcome of a problem. We memorized formulas. We spent countless hours solving for X, and while I may never use $y = mx + b$ in my everyday life, I'm sure I will be able to recite it on my deathbed.

In motherhood, one of the most important formulas to be aware of is the formula for "Hangry." Take your child out to run errands. Forget to pack snacks. End up staying out past lunchtime. Add in a "no" to something they've asked for, and there you have it. Hangry. And if you want to get a little wild and crazy, start these errands when your child is already tired. Putting this into algebraic terms would look something like this:

$$H(t) = dt - e$$

Here, H is hangry, d is the toddler's desire for something, t is the length of time it has been since they last ate, and *e* is their emotional maturity. The variables may change, but the outcome is always the same: Hangry.

The hangry phenomenon should obviously be avoided at all costs. Once kids cross the hangry threshold, it is not pretty. As mothers, we spend ninety-two percent of our time juggling all these variables in order to maintain a reasonably happy outcome.

Multiplication and Exponential Growth

Mathematics also taught us all about multiplication, and that is, after all, what we are doing when we have children. We are multiplying ourselves, fulfilling that age-old creation mandate.

When my husband and I were dating, he told me he wanted a large family. At that moment, my heart fluttered because so did I. I'd always wanted a larger family like the four-kid family I'd grown up in, but it turns out, *large* is a vague and relative term because *large* to him, I found out within a few months, meant more like ten kids. Ten! I must have really been in love because I did not turn and run for the hills right then and there.

My husband has a pretty high tolerance for crazy, but now that we are a few kids in, I think even he has given up on his dream of enough kids for a five-on-five basketball scrimmage. We won't be getting a TLC reality show because when you continue to multiply yourself, you continue to multiply other things too. You multiply the dishes, the chaos, the hangry meltdowns.

And the laundry! The laundry actually grows exponentially with the addition of each child. I'm really not sure if we can have any more kids simply because I'm not sure that I can manage any more laundry. Perhaps after you have a certain number of children, you come up with a new system, like each family member only gets to wear pants on Tuesdays and Thursdays. Or maybe everyone has to wear the same clothes at least two days in a row. Let's be honest. That happens sometimes anyway.

Love Multiplied

It's no doubt that when you become a mom, the equations in your life become a lot more complex. Multiplying ourselves seems to mean we add more laundry and stress, double our grocery budget, and divide our sleep in half. And time alone? That's basically in negative numbers. It's a lot to handle, but as we grow as mothers, we find that we can juggle more than we thought we could. We can survive and even thrive with less sleep. We can balance more variables. And while it's true that as we add more children we multiply the difficult things, we also multiply the blessings: the love, the joy, the fun. The more these little people grow, the more our hearts expand to take it all in.

Before my oldest child was born, he was an

abstract idea. Afterward, he became a concrete reality of projectile poop and middle-of-the-night scream sessions. Sleeping is one of my favorite things, and suddenly I was sleeping in one-hour stretches and nodding off during feedings. I remember taking my brand new baby to Walmart when he was a few weeks old and trudging around the store in a zombie-like haze. I was so tired that I thought I might fall asleep mid-step, right there in the frozen food aisle.

Of course, I loved him right away, but new motherhood kind of hit me upside the head like a ton of bricks. My world was completely shattered, and I struggled to accept how much my life now revolved around another totally helpless person.

Then one day, a few weeks into sleep deprivation, I was rocking my son. His eyes locked with mine, and he smiled at me. In that moment, I was what we call a "goner" and right then and there I fell completely in love. With each child, I have fallen in love all over again.

So there I was with this new little person added, sleep subtracted, and love multiplied. I remember almost feeling overcome by this big love. The thought that kept circulating through my mind was, *I've never been so certain I would die for someone.* I think we all hope that we'll be that courageous, selfless person who jumps in front of another to take the bullet, but we never know for sure unless we are put in that situation. When it comes to my kids, though, I just know.

I know I wouldn't hesitate, not for a moment, to give my life for theirs.

This is love. It's the great love Jesus spoke about in the Gospel of John, saying "Greater love has no one than this, that someone lay down his life for his friends" (John 15:13). Motherhood is the closest I've come to understanding the love of God, and it's still only the faintest whisper. As sinful, selfish human beings, we fall short of practicing this great love daily, but when we have children, I think we get a little closer.

We are still only finite beings, so we can talk about the concept of infinity, or God's limitless love, but it is ever shrouded in mystery. By definition, infinite love is beyond our reach. I remember spending a lot of time in calculus class finding limits as *X* approached infinity: *X* was desperate to get there even though there is no *there*. You can't find the end of something that has no end. You can't fully understand something that goes on forever. The Bible tells us God's love is like that. Infinite. Incomprehensible. Unquantifiable.

Think back to the Garden of Eden. Only a few chapters into the Bible, things go terribly wrong there. God had created man and woman. He had created a luscious, beautiful paradise for them to live in. And He, God Himself, dwelled with them.

He had one rule—just *one*. They were allowed to eat from any tree except one—just *one*. It sounds simple enough. Risking death for a piece of fruit definitely seems foolish to me. A juicy steak fresh off the grill? Maybe. But, of course, there was more to it than the fruit. It was the lie behind the fruit—the lie that God was not truly, infinitely loving and good. Adam and Eve chose to believe the lie. They chose to be disobedient children. Sin and death came on the scene.

How did God respond? He responded as the perfect Father. Perfectly merciful and just, He announced the due penalties for their sin and their upcoming departure from Eden and communion with Himself, yet He also announced His plan to get them back. He didn't curse them and walk away. He didn't wipe them out of existence and start over as He would have been perfectly justified in doing. He brought justice but also a glimmer of grace.

Listen for it as God spoke to the serpent. He said, "I will put enmity between you and the woman, and between your offspring and her offspring; he shall bruise your head, and you shall bruise his heel" (Genesis 3:15).

Did you catch it? Did you hear the very first whisper of Jesus? Death had come to His children, and God declared His plan to take that death upon Himself on the cross. He didn't have to think about it. He didn't have to weigh his options and decide if they were worth it. No, although Adam and Eve were headed for death, Jesus stepped up and said, "I will take their place. I will pay the price that they may live."

In the greatest of inverse relationships, the less worthy of love they became, the more Jesus loved them. The Bible says this is how we know what love is: "that He laid down his life for us" (1 John 3:16).

The Burden of Love

Most of us have an innate sense that love is the most important force in the universe, but if we forsake its Source, we lack the ability to truly understand it. In movies or songs, love is usually made out to be a feeling or an emotional high, but as mothers, we know that love is made of much weightier stuff. Love is carefully cutting grapes into fourths. It's getting up five times a night or catching vomit in your hands. We know that to truly love someone can be a burden.

We have a vision for our children's lives. Things we hope they will learn and do along with things we hope they will not learn or do. We hope they won't repeat our mistakes, like wearing brightly patterned wind suits, or staying out late with friends instead of studying for their physics final, or dating the completely wrong person. We sometimes wish we had a time machine so that they could skip the unique and painful awkwardness of seventh grade. There are pitfalls and painful experiences we pray they will avoid, but we know that things will not work out according to our plans.

Inevitably, our children will encounter struggles.

They will make mistakes and get hurt. Others will hurt them. They will even hurt us. They could reject God just as Adam and Eve did that fateful day. Their lives could end early and so bring tragedy and sorrow to ours.

As C. S. Lewis said in *The Four Loves*, "To love at all is to be vulnerable. Love anything, and your heart will certainly be wrung and possibly be broken. If you want to make sure of keeping it intact, you must give your heart to no one."[1] Love can be painful and costly because when we love, we open ourselves to the pain and grief of another. Their ache becomes our ache. Their loss becomes our loss. To love someone is to carry their burdens as your own. I was terrifyingly aware of this in those early years with my firstborn. I had never felt so completely vulnerable.

I can't forget the first time I watched my son get his feelings hurt. He was about two-and-a-half. We were at a backyard cookout, and the older kids turned up their noses at him and told him he couldn't play with them. He turned away a little sadly, but moved on quickly—I felt like my heart had been torn in two. If it hurt so much to watch that, how will I be able to handle watching him fail to make the football team or be rejected by a girl? Maybe I could arrange a marriage so he can skip the cycle of crushes and rejection to which I may or may not have devoted several high school diaries.

---

1. C.S. Lewis, *The Beloved Works of C.S. Lewis* (NY: Inspirational Press, 2004), 278-279.

When I became a mother, I felt this overwhelming love, this sense of excitement to see my son's life unfold, but right alongside it, this sense of fear. He seemed so small and the world so big. There were millions of ways it could all go wrong, millions of ways he could get hurt. I knew that meant I would hurt too.

At times I've wondered why God created mankind, knowing all along how humans would reject Him and the pain it would cause Him, how He would have to suffer for them. God wasn't surprised we chose sin. He knew. He knew it would hurt to love us. I can't pretend to know God's mind, but I think I understand it a little better now than I did before having kids. Even though I realize how loving my children could bring me pain, I know I would never want to erase their lives to avoid it. Knowing them and loving them is an unqualified good.

I think that's a little of how God feels about His children. He created us, not because He lacked anything or needed us, but because He wanted us—even knowing all the ways we would fail. God "does all that He pleases" (Psalm 115:3). It pleased Him to make us, and it pleased Him to save us. Burdened by love, He became the most vulnerable thing on earth: a baby. Though we rejected Him, He embraced pain and sorrow to save us. And His love for His children cost Him his life.

Having a child means we wade a little deeper into

that kind of love. The more children we add, the more it multiplies. Maybe we're knee-deep in laundry, and maybe our children have turned our once simple, straightforward lives into a complex math equation, but when we look at them, we know we're in this all the way. Whatever it takes, we pray we can love them as Christ has loved us, embracing the pain as well as the joy, counting the cost as well as the blessing.

Reflection Questions

1) This chapter describes God's relationship with Adam and Eve this way: "In the greatest of inverse relationships, the less worthy of love they became, the more Jesus loved them." Think of specific times and ways God has loved you when you were not worthy of love. Thank Him for His love.

2) Real love is costly, and sometimes hard. In what ways have you experienced this truth as a mother? What are specific ways you can take steps to better reflect God's love to your kids?

3) God chose to create mankind knowing exactly what it would cost Him to love us. Read Psalm 103:8-13 and Romans 5:6-8 and reflect on the perfect, limitless love of God for *you*.

2

Physics

Laws and Limits under an Infinite God

The love of a mother is a powerful force, and it can seem like your cute, little, squishy baby could never possibly do anything besides melt your heart into a puddle. But if you've made it through the baby phase and passed into the toddler years, you know that some days are not quite as endearing. You've traded the endless diaper changing for, well, more endless diaper changing plus a side of attitude . . . that is, unless, you've decided to brave the yellow waters of potty-training, which just means scrubbing urine puddles off the floor with that same side of attitude. If you've found that your happy, likeable child has now begun a long-term relationship with the word *no*, you will need to understand a few laws of physics—toddler physics.

Toddlers are marvelous creatures. They are cute—and I mean, really, really cute. You thought babies couldn't get any cuter, but they can. Yet, you fawn over your toddler's over-sized Disney eyes one moment and pull your hair out the next as said toddler decides to cut his own hair (right in the front), or decorate her walls with abstract art, or throw all your toothbrushes in the toilet. Toddlers are little people with big emotions and a *very* small capacity for reason.

You will find yourself trying to explain things to them, down to basic facts of life—why the sky is blue, why the red cup is as good as the blue cup, why they can't eat butter for lunch, or why they shouldn't throw blocks by the baby. You will try to use logic, but it will be like trying to teach algebra to a rock—only worse, because at least rocks don't cry.

And don't get me started on choices. Toddlers are notoriously bad decision makers. Even if presented with all the facts, eight different ways, in PowerPoint presentations complete with graphs and data, they will still frequently, if not always, make the wrong choice. For example, you will say things like, "If you throw that sippy cup one more time, I'm going to take it." Sounds simple enough, right? The correct choice seems obvious, yet they will throw the sippy cup one more time and then pitch the fit of the decade when you confiscate it, despite your perfectly lucid explanation of cause and effect.

Toddler Physics

These kinds of interactions happen daily in life with a toddler, which means the laws of physics are quite relevant to this season of motherhood. But have no fear, because I'm keeping this simple—physics and I did not get along, so I don't remember much, but I do recall Newton's third law of motion: for every action, there is an equal and opposite reaction.

Toddler physics illustrates this law perfectly, except with a twist: in the toddler universe, for every action, there is an equal and opposite *over*reaction. Did your toddler drop his fork from the highchair? He had planned on being buried with that very fork. Tears are now necessary to mourn its loss. Did your toddler's shoe come off? That day and probably all the rest of her days are effectively ruined. Nothing could possibly rectify this, and if you dare suggest that she simply put her shoe back on, watch out. Did you tell your toddler that he could not play with the knives? He will promptly conclude that you never really loved him. Cue epic meltdown over his tragically knife-less existence.

Every slightly negative experience in the toddler universe is the end of all possible goodness. I repeat: big emotions, itty-bitty reasoning capacity.

In college, I studied philosophy, which literally means the love of reason, so spending my days with people who seem allergic to it is especially exhausting. I know they will develop a taste for it, but those days sometimes seem so far away—these days require patience. Go in the closet and scream if you need to, but keep teaching them calmly, one day at a time. Someday the rock will grow up and learn to reason, and you will regain your sanity … or at least what's left of it.

Space and Time

Physics is the study of space and time, but as your child becomes a toddler, you will quickly learn that children have no sense of space—personal space, that is. Especially when the personal space belongs to their moms. Only yesterday, my two-year-old climbed into my lap while I was going to the bathroom, studied the situation, and then told me, "Good job, Mommy!"

I'll be sure to put "pees in potty" on my résumé.

Toddlers also have little to no real grasp of the concept of time. You see, when you've been on the earth for about the same time as some fruit flies, minutes are like years, and hours are like eons. Just as toddlers have no capacity to understand cause and effect, neither do they have any ability to comprehend words like *before* or *after* or *later*, and certainly not *next week.*

Here's what you need to know. Do not ever under any circumstances tell your toddler that you are going to do something until you are doing it. Is Grandma coming on Thursday? Do not mention it on Monday unless you want to hear about Grandma for all of Tuesday and Wednesday. And expect at least one crying fit when the toddler realizes that Thursday is not today, because so far as she can imagine, if it's not happening right now, it will never happen.

I recently told my two-year-old that we were going to a birthday party later that day. This was a rookie mistake that I, as a seasoned—well, lightly seasoned—mother of four should have known not to make. Yet there I was in the store blathering on about the birthday party. Never underestimate the singular focus of a two-year-old. I did not stop hearing "Why aren't we going to the party?" for hours, even after I explained and re-explained that the party was *later*.

Just know that these time-related words mean absolutely nothing to your toddler unless they're measured in "sleeps" or *Paw Patrol* episodes. The only time they comprehend is now, so unless you are ready to do it *now*, save yourself the agony, and keep the surprises to yourself.

Bending the Laws of Physics

Some shock waves are inevitable, though. Sometimes, motherhood requires you to do things that you never thought you could do. You will need to push the boundaries of what you thought humanly possible. And if your family grows through the addition of children, you will get better at this out of survival necessity.

For example, maybe you didn't think you could discipline your tantrum-throwing toddler at thirty-nine weeks pregnant, but then you managed it. Maybe you didn't think you could breastfeed your baby *and* refill your toddler's juice cup at the same time, but look at you go. I don't know if I'm proud or embarrassed to admit this, but I once nursed my son *while he was in his car seat* and we were stuck in traffic. I never knew

I could bend that way, but the kid was hungry and the cars were not moving. What was a mom to do?

Fingers crossed I didn't give Highway 635 a show they weren't asking for.

Moms make possible things that seem impossible. We get it done because we must. I don't like calling moms superheroes because we're not. We're just everyday heroes who wear three-day-old t-shirts instead of capes and who daily push the boundaries of sleep-deprivation, personal hygiene, and multi-tasking to take care of little people we love.

Facing Our Limits

Of course, all of this means that at some point, we do reach the boundaries of what we can do. Physics teaches us that we are bound by certain laws. I can't lift a car off the ground because my muscles lack the power needed to counter the car's gravitational force. Certain things simply are not possible, and there is nothing like motherhood to teach us the same thing. Motherhood shows us our limits. In fact, it took less than a week of motherhood to meet one of my limits. Maybe that's a record low.

I had been a mother for only five days. Five days with my precious newborn. Five days with essentially no sleep. On the sixth day, my husband and I stumbled into the ER around 4:00 am because my son hadn't had any wet diapers in twenty-four hours. I was new to the job, but I did remember from the classes that twenty-four hours of dry diapers was too long. He'd been nursing for long periods, so I assumed that meant he was getting plenty to eat, I explained through yawns to the doctors.

Mercifully, the doctor was a woman and a mom of three. She watched me nurse and then kindly explained to me that my son wasn't latching correctly. He was nursing for so long because he wasn't actually getting any nutrition. In my near comatose state, I'd had no idea that I was breastfeeding wrong. I felt like a terrible mom for not knowing, but I also felt like I might die if I didn't sleep soon. In fact, I laid down on the patient table right there and fell asleep while the nurse fed my son a bottle of formula.

Five days. That's all it took for me to meet my physical limits. Superhuman strength and clarity would be super helpful in motherhood, but apparently these aren't among the spiritual gifts. We are human and therefore finite. Coming to terms with our limitations as parents can be humbling and terrifying, and that is exactly why we need to talk about the big fear.

If you knew what I meant about the big love in chapter one, then you'll also know what I mean about the big fear. It's the feeling that grips your heart when you read that headline about a perfectly healthy four-year-old dying from the flu. That could be your own perfectly healthy four-year-old. Or it's the story someone shared on Facebook about the newborn who got kissed by a stranger and then got herpes and died. That could be your newborn. Or the news segment on secondary drowning. Forget normal drowning. Now we also worry about *secondary* drowning. Better steer clear of all bodies of water and maybe even baths.

Everywhere we turn, there are things to fear.

C. S. Lewis was right when he said the fear and the love go hand in hand because once we have something to love, we know we also have something to lose. We know we are vulnerable to pain. The big fear accompanied me on the drive home from the hospital with my first son. We had to take the highway. Until that moment, I'd never realized what crazy death traps highways are. I felt like we needed a police escort to announce to all of the maniacs on the road that we were carrying this impossibly tiny, fragile person, and that they all needed to slow down. My husband was driving like a grandpa, but it still seemed too fast. *We should probably just drive twenty miles an hour from here on out*, I thought. I sat in the back, next to the car seat, as if my closeness could protect him should we get in an accident. I am not a large person and once lost an arm-wrestling match to my eighty-seven-year-old grandmother (she's freakishly strong, okay?), but I was fully prepared to be a human shield for my son.

Those first nights at home, when we'd finally gotten our son to sleep, I would lie there and listen for every possible tiny movement or sound he made. Did he cough? Is he choking? Before we'd left the hospital with him, a seasoned nurse had nonchalantly told me to watch out in case he choked on amniotic fluid. "Push this button and say 'baby choking,'" she said, almost as an afterthought as she left my room. So, naturally, I began standing guard over my newborn's every waking and sleeping moment.

At home, though, there was no button to push or nurse to call for help. Apparently, when we signed up to be parents, we signed up to be solely responsible for things like choking. Who knew? Maybe we should have done a lower-stakes test run with something like a puppy ... or a goldfish. But there we were with a tiny baby who somehow was supposed to breathe on his own. I would often find myself unable to sleep at night, getting up just to make sure he was breathing.

When our son was a few weeks old, a man from Africa had flown to Dallas, a mere thirty-minute drive from our house, and gotten sick with Ebola. *Ebola!* Then, one of the nurses at the hospital treating him got it. Then *another* nurse got it. I read this headline while I was up nursing at 4:00 a.m.—you know, when my brain was at its most rational. As I crawled back into bed, I woke my husband to inform him that this was clearly an epidemic spreading mere miles from my tiny son with his no-good immune system. I conclud-ed, of course, that we needed to run away to a bunker in the woods—somewhere far away from Ebola and anything else that might harm our baby boy.

This is the big fear; it is as powerful as the big love, and if we let it, it will consume us. It will drive us mad because there is nothing we can do and nowhere we can run to make sure that our children are *one hundred percent safe*. We can and should do everything in our power to guard them. We put them in car seats to protect them from the potential force of impact in a car crash. We put them in swim floaties to buoy them up and make them light enough to float. We cut their grapes into tiny pieces so they won't choke. Yet none of this guarantees safety. This world is a dangerous place, and we must learn how to live in it without losing our minds.

The question is, how? How do we live in this world, loving these little people with this big love, and not go completely insane with this big fear?

It starts with theology.

Yes, that's right. Theology. The study of God. Because what we believe about God will determine how we deal with our fear and how we come to terms with our limitations as finite people bound in space and time.

Surrendered to Sovereignty

In all of those first moments with my first child, from hovering over him on the highway to listening to his every sound as he slept, I was trying to be superhuman—to be everywhere and to protect him from everything. Essentially, I wanted to be God.

Of course, that quickly fell apart because, as it turns out, I am not God, and I need a good night's sleep just to be a decent version of myself. I remember the Lord's loving, gentle admonition speaking into my exhaustion. I was holding my son after nursing and feeling that big love right alongside that big fear that often accompanied it. I wondered, *what if something happened to him?* God reminded me of Colossians 1:17, which describes the sustaining power of Jesus: "And He is before all things, and in Him all things hold together." Not only did God create my son, but He also held every atom of my son's body together at every moment. My son's heart would not miss one beat apart from God's will.

In my fear, I attempted to carry a burden I was never asked to carry. I took it as my job to keep my son alive. And in a sense, it was. We *are* responsible to do our very best to care for our children, which includes keeping them alive to the best of our abilities, but their safety ultimately lies beyond our complete control. We do not have that kind of power. Only God does. God is responsible for whether our children live or die. God is sovereign over their lives, not us. This is both relieving and terrifying. The terrifying part is that someone else besides us is in control of what happens to them ... and the relieving part is that someone else besides us is in control of what happens to them. We can rest in the good news that the someone else in control is God, and because he is unlimited in power and knowledge and presence, he is far better equipped to take the helm than we limited humans.

Motherhood forced me to surrender myself to the truth of God's sovereignty in a way that I never had to do before. It forced me to consider if I really believed in my heart the theology I knew in my head. Did I really believe that God was reigning and ruling? And if I did, did I really trust that He was the best one to be reigning and ruling? (Hint: my plans to live in a bunker after the Ebola scare indicated my answer to these questions was no).

My fear told me that the world is a dangerous, haphazard place. And truthfully, it often looks that way, like chaos and senselessness reign, like there is no orderly kingdom ruled by a loving God. But having faith as a mother is about believing what our eyes can't see: that God is sovereign over every danger and threat, big or small.

I remember the fear I felt the first time my son got sick. Looking back, I was definitely overreacting—not quite fork-dropped-by-toddler overreacting, but overreacting nonetheless. My child had a cold and an ear infection, which to me as a first-time mom may as well have been scarlet fever. For thousands of years, human biology had proven fairly successful in fighting off colds, almost as if it was designed to do so, but I couldn't be sure in this instance. On the drive to the doctor, I could feel the fear rising, and I prayed out loud, reminding myself of the truths I knew. God was sovereign over all. He upheld the universe and He also upheld every cell of my son's little body. Not only that, but He loved both me and my son enough to send *His* son to die for us.

As I gripped the steering wheel and spoke these truths, God calmed my heart. His perfect love cast out my fear. He reminded me that He is the God of Isaiah 40, "the Lord God who comes with might" (verse 10) as well as the Shepherd who carries the lambs and leads their mothers with gentleness (verse 11). He is a God who is both wonderfully transcendent and immanent. The laws of physics constrain us, but they do not constrain Him.

This great, sovereign, transcendent God created the world, and He reigns over the world. He created our children, and He reigns over our children. His eye is on the sparrow, and His eye is on young mothers. Nothing escapes His notice or His reach. Neither does anything escape His care. Not an exhausted mom falling asleep on a crinkly-papered ER table or a scared mom driving her baby to the doctor for the first sick visit. The perfect Shepherd walks closely with His weak and needy sheep, gently leading us as we lead our young, even while He causes the sun to rise on our earth each day and keeps the planets spinning in their orbits.

When we are faced with scary circumstances, we are tempted to live as if we are sovereign and not God. This ironically doesn't free us from our fears but shackles us to them. We don't need more control to conquer fear. We need a renewed vision of God. We need to lift our eyes off our fears and fix them on Him. We need to ask as the Psalmist did, "Where does my help come from?" (Psalm 121:2). It does not come from the worn copy of *What to Expect When You're Expecting* or having your pediatrician as #1 on speed dial, or all the expert articles on baby-proofing your home. Our help comes from God, who, in His goodness, will always answer us with the truth we desperately need. He will show us who He is as He showed me that day in the car.

The Bible tells us that God is intimately involved with His creation. From the supernovas of the cosmos to the inner workings of the tiniest parts of a cell, God is there holding it all together (Colossians 1:17). He is just as intimately involved with our children. He knows the overarching story of their lives, and He knows every hair on their heads. Psalm 127:1 says that "Unless the Lord watches over the city, the watchmen stand guard in vain." It doesn't say, "so don't watch over the city." It doesn't say, "God is in charge, so go have a siesta." It's a call to vigilantly watch over the city, yet to rest our souls in the truth that there is someone greater watching over it all.

We can (and should) take all the proper safety precautions, but even if we do everything in our power to keep our children from harm, they may yet be harmed. Some things are simply out of our control, but they are not out of God's. We can trust Him to watch over our children when we can't. We can sleep because we know He won't (Psalm 121:4). Freedom from fear starts with surrendering ourselves and our children to the One who reigns.

Rejoicing in Sovereignty

Loving our children makes us vulnerable to pain, and surrendering to the sovereignty of God doesn't change that. That surrender liberates us from the burden of trying to be God, but it gives us a different burden: the burden of loving what we know God may take away.

Our sovereign God has not promised that nothing we fear will happen to our children. We would do well to take careful stock of what God has actually promised us, not what we think He *should* promise us. We will all encounter loss and suffering in this life. Some of us may encounter more than others. We may say with Job, "The thing I fear comes upon me, and what I dread befalls me" (Job 3:25). Our worst fears really could come about. That is the plain truth. But here is another truth: *nothing* will happen apart from the sovereign will and decree of God.

Though suffering and grief may come, we are not victims of blind, unfeeling chance. As Jerry Bridges so aptly wrote,

> God does as He pleases, only as He pleases, and works out every event to bring about the accomplishment of His will. Such a bare unqualified statement of the sovereignty of God would terrify us if that were all we knew about God. But God is not only sovereign, He is perfect in love and infinite in wisdom.[2]

Every moment is governed by God, and this God is good. He is wise. He is loving. He is mighty. Anything less, and He could not be trusted. Should He be loving but not wise, He could make mistakes. Should He be wise but not mighty, He could be unable to do what's best. Should He be mighty but not good, He could choose to work things for our harm.

Yet, He is loving *and* wise *and* mighty *and* good. How do we know? We know Jesus. In sending Jesus, God showed us that He knew exactly what needed to be done to save us. And when Jesus died on the cross, He showed us that He loved us enough to do what needed to be done. Rising from the dead, Jesus

---

2. Jerry Bridges, *Trusting God* (Colorado Springs: NavPress, 2008), 35.

showed us He also had enough power to accomplish what needed to be done. Then, when Jesus ascended into heaven, He promised to go and prepare a place for us, a place where every tear will be wiped away, every wrong made right, every hurt redeemed.

This is the God who reigns over us and over our children. He doesn't promise us no pain, no loss. But if we are in Christ, He does promise to work all things for our good (Romans 8:28). Bridges again assures us, "Because we are united with Christ, whatever is for His glory is also for our good. And whatever is for our good is for His glory."[3] No pain will enter our lives without His good purpose. No loss will come apart from His wisdom and power. And in the end, all will be redeemed and made new by the power and might and grace of our risen Savior.

Mothers, God's sovereignty isn't merely true. It is the good news that God is ultimately in control and we are not. You and I are bound by the laws of physics, and we would do well to accept our limitations while trusting the God who has none. When you see a headline or read a story on Facebook that wraps your heart in fear, tell your fear about your God. Use all your means and your knowledge to keep your children safe, but trust God to be God. Don't let fear rule your motherhood, but surrender it to the One who rules over all.

---

3. Jerry Bridges, *Trusting God* (Colorado Springs: NavPress, 2008), 140.

Reflection Questions

1) List specific fears you wrestle with as a mother that tempt you to try to "play God." Does playing God produce the peace and sense of security we want?

2) Think of how right theology and the doctrine of God's sovereignty speaks to your specific fears. Choose a verse or phrase you can meditate on and even say out loud to "speak back" to your fears when they arise. Maybe even write it down on a sticky note and place it where you can see it in the moment you need it.

3) "We don't need more control to conquer fear. We need a renewed vision of God." Read Isaiah 40, which invites us, which commands us, which calls out to us, "Behold your God!" As you read, reflect on how God is with us in our day to day—bandaging scraped knees and administering Tylenol to feverish babies—even while He also upholds the entire universe. How does this reveal Him as trustworthy?

3

Language Skills

Toddler-ese and the Vocabulary of Sacrifice

If you went to high school, then like me, you may have had to take a language. If you were also like me and wanted to satisfy your language requirement in the easiest way possible, you took Spanish, unlike the overachievers, who took classes like Latin or German. Either way, I now only remember as much Spanish as I know German: *eins, zwei, drei... uno, dos, tres...*

I have no regrets about letting my Spanish competency drop to barely being able to understand those *Yo Quiero Taco Bell* commercials, but I do regret not becoming fluent in another language: toddler. That's because toddlers have their own language, and it is complex. In fact, *each* individual toddler has his or her own language. As your particular toddler's mother, you will need to become fluent in this language in order to attempt to communicate with your child. If your toddler is like my first son, who was a bit slow to talk and had a slight speech impediment, you may even have to learn a language that sounds to a native English speaker as foreign and uninterpretable as Japanese.

One great thing about the toddler phase is that your child will inevitably turn innocent words like *truck* or *frog* into profanities, and it will be the funniest thing in the world. To the untrained ear, it sounded like my son was running around excitedly insulting everyone when he was merely exclaiming "dump truck!" This is the only time it will be appropriate to laugh and take a video when your child swears, so enjoy.

But just as only you really know what your child is saying in the produce aisle, you will also, in time, get so used to your child's language that it will seem completely normal, and you will forget that other people don't speak it. Your kid will run around yelling "Namala! Namala!" And you will not understand why Grandma can't figure out that your child is yelling excitedly about the "lawnmower" he spotted across the street. Come on, Grandma. But Grandma and everyone else in the world will look at your child with a blank stare. You will have to translate these things for others because they do not speak your child's particular dialect of Toddler-ese.

Even though you will become skilled at interpreting most of the things your child says, there will inevitably be times when even you cannot guess what in the world they are saying. They will get frustrated that you do not understand what they believe they are very clearly saying. After asking "what?" a few times, you may give up because you can't figure it out and are too distracted or lazy to keep trying. You will come up with some generic response that will hopefully satisfy them like "Okay, great" or "Sure, baby," vaguely hoping that they weren't saying something like "When I grow up I want to work at Hooters," or "Can I paint the bathroom walls with your nail polish?"

Eventually, your child will become more intelligible. They will stop speaking their particular brand of gibberish, and while it will be much easier to converse, you will miss the way they mispronounced some words and the way mixed all their Cs for Ts. They will become well-spoken, articulate little people who are surprisingly good at arguing their way into having pizza for lunch again, and this will be yet another bittersweet symptom of what we call "growing up," a malady that afflicts them all.

While our children's language becomes more advanced as time passes, it might seem that ours become less so. Because when we become moms, the language we use changes too. I sometimes find it difficult to put sentences together because my brain is on complete overload. I now understand why my mother often called me the wrong name when I was a kid.

She called me Henry.

Henry was our dog.

After suffering this grave indignity for years, I

swore I would never mix up my kids' names, but alas, here I am, regularly calling my children by every name but their own. Half the time I give up and say, "Oh whoever you are!" in lieu of their beautiful names, which my husband and I spent months debating on prior to their births. I guess it's good we don't have a dog yet. And then sometimes when I do manage to get the right words out, I'm amazed at what they are. "Don't lick the shower!" "Why did you pee in the refrigerator?" These sentences, and others just as odd, have actually left my mouth, leaving me to wonder—*what even is my life?*

We may marvel at how we arrived at a point where we frequently exhort people to stop eating the garbage. Once upon a time in our carefree youth, we chatted with our friends about school or work, maybe even the latest big movie or book. Now we text about baby food or the best deal for diapers. Once upon a time, we sat in college classrooms and debated with peers about the Revolutionary War or Aristotle. Now we sit in our kitchens and debate with our two-year-olds about why they can't eat the entire stick of butter or lick the salt shaker.

Before I had kids, I spent one semester in graduate school. The professor of my hardest class had a German accent and glasses—everything you would think a philosophy professor would be. I was intimidated by the other people in the class who used words like *poiesis* and *epiphenomenal* with ease and frequency. I wrote the longest, hardest paper I ever had to write for that class. Here's a snippet:

> As already shown, MacIntyre rejected encyclopaedia as a form of moral enquiry because it was based on the false assumption of universal reason. He also proposed ways in which the tradition of Thomism explains the inadequacies of encyclopaedia so as to demonstrate its rational superiority.

Riveting, I know. But I understood what those sentences meant when I composed them for that class. Now, the same person sings "The B-I-B-LE" about twenty times a day, per my toddler's demands. And I could write you a thousand words on diaper rash treatment in my sleep.

I feel the loss of it sometimes—the loss of that version of myself who could hold a conversation about deep things and write about them with reasonable credibility. It's not that she's totally gone. But she's definitely out of practice, the language of philosophy currently drowned out by the language of motherhood. Motherhood changes almost everything about our lives—how we dress, what we eat or drink, where we go, what we think about. We inevitably give some things up—even what we talk about and how we talk about it. Motherhood is nothing if not sacrifice.

The Sacrifice of Motherhood

I once wrote an online piece about some of the sacrifices that come with being a mom. Most people found it encouraging, but one man offered strong negative comments. He was "outraged" and said that motherhood is a blessing and, therefore, never a sacrifice (a little ironic considering his gender and his complete lack of experience as a mother). The main objective of the piece was to display the beauty and purpose of motherhood despite—and sometimes because of—its struggles, so I was a little bothered by his harsh words.

I have three sisters who are all in the thick of motherhood with me, and we joke about this man a lot. We remind each other that we're never allowed to call anything about motherhood hard or unpleasant. One of my sisters recently had a hysterectomy because of the physical damage she experienced from carrying four babies. She literally had an organ cut out of her body, but we made sure to tell her, "Remember, Beth: this is *not* a sacrifice."

When that man commented on my piece online, I decided it would be wise not to respond, but there have been many times since that I wish I had responded—not to defend myself personally or to complain, but to defend a beautiful truth. Because in some difficult moments, I have thought, *This is absolutely sacrifice*, and that has helped me persevere. Like the times I emptied my lunch in the toilet during my first trimester, and it splashed me in the face. Like when my children have awakened me in the middle of the night, and I have slept on the floor to be nearby when they have fever. Like when my back has ached from caring for my toddlers all day while also carrying another in my womb, or when I dealt with depression a few months after my third baby was born. These are only a few examples of the ways all moms sacrifice for their kids—and many moms sacrifice much, much more. Are these sacrifices small in the grand scheme of things? Yes, many of them are. Do we bear these sacrifices gladly? Yes—we want to do so, anyway. Does any of that mean that these are not real hardships? Definitely not.

I want to be absolutely clear. Motherhood is the greatest blessing and privilege of my life. I know there are many women who have lost a child or struggle with infertility who would give anything to be in my vomit-covered shoes. I can only imagine that kind of pain, and I never want to complain. All the sacrifices I have made, which are relatively small, are nothing compared to the joy of mothering my children. But just because motherhood is a joy doesn't mean every second of it *feels* joyful. Nor does it mean that motherhood doesn't demand very real, and sometimes very difficult, sacrifice.

The Language of Sacrifice

From the second we see those two pink lines, mothers begin sacrificing for our children.

We give up certain foods and drinks. We give up big things like having our bodies to ourselves and small things like sleeping on our backs at night. That's the simple truth. Being honest about that truth does not denigrate motherhood. Rather, it magnifies the beauty and worth of motherhood. Calling something a sacrifice doesn't make it a negative thing. It makes it a beautiful thing.

The word *sacrifice* merely means relinquishing something to gain something else. We don't call it *sacrifice* when we give up something we don't want, nor do we *sacrifice* for something we don't value. But we make sacrifices because we value what we get more than what we lose. Runners endure hours of training, pain, and struggle because they value the reward of finishing a race well. Students aiming for good grades gives up socializing on the weekends. Married people give up certain freedoms and take on more responsibilities because they love and value their commitment to their spouses.

In the same way, when we give up things for our children—our time, our energy, our personal comfort, our preferences, even our very bodies—we essentially declare to our children: "I cherish you more than a good night's sleep. I'd rather have you than a perfect home or a glamorous career. I want you more than I want a perfect body or even a healthy, pain-free body. You are worth far more to me than all these things." Motherhood speaks the language of sacrifice to our children and to the world.

To love other people is to give them a claim on your life, to voluntarily relinquish and restrict your freedoms and comforts for their sake. That's what motherhood is. Calling it a sacrifice does not diminish its inherent beauty and worth but *enhances* it.

In its Latin roots, the word *sacrifice* breaks down into *sacer*, which means *holy*, and *facere*, which means *to make*. Are you seeing this? The literal meaning of *sacrifice* has nothing to do with pain or hardship or loss. It literally means *to make holy*.

Motherhood is a holy endeavor not because we *are* holy—just ask my husband who overheard me yelling at my kids about the half-eaten bananas I keep finding all over the house—but because motherhood itself *makes* us holy. How does it do that? The sacrifice that is motherhood makes us holy because it makes us more like Jesus, the expert in sacrifice.

For mothers, sacrifice looks like giving up a good night's sleep (or the ability to drop phrases like "inadequacies of encyclopaedia") but for Jesus it looked like giving up a throne of endless glory. He gave up heaven to become a human for us. He gave up His absolute right to condemn us as Judge and surrendered His own life to pay for our sins. For us and "for the joy that was set before Him" (Hebrews 12:2), He literally *became* a sacrifice ... because He loved us more than He loved His rights, His body, His very life. We were worth more to Him than all these things. He died to make us His children, to present us blameless before the Father, and to bring eternal praise and glory to God.

Motherhood is a holy calling because it is a calling to be like Jesus. Acknowledging the sacrifices of motherhood is not a hindrance to this calling. It is the essence of it.

Sacrifice as Worship

In the book of Romans, the apostle Paul gives us the most masterful, compelling account of the theology of the gospel. The Christian hears of the condemnation and death from sin, the shocking love and forgiveness of God, and the unshakable assurance that God will work all things together for their good. Then in chapter twelve, based on all of these marvelous truths, Paul makes an important appeal.

> I appeal to you therefore, brothers, by the mercies of God, to present your bodies as a living sacrifice, holy and acceptable to God, which is your spiritual worship. Do not be conformed to this world, but be transformed by the renewal of your mind, that by testing you may discern what is

> the will of God, what is good and acceptable and perfect. (Romans 12:1–2)

Do you catch the logic here? Paul has just given the Romans a beautiful, theologically profound view of the overarching mercy of God displayed most keenly in the sacrifice of Christ for sinners. Those who truly see this astounding mercy have only one proper response, and that is worship. What is the substance of this worship? It is not only words sung on Sundays; it is self-sacrifice.

In the thick of motherhood, we can easily forget what may seem like lofty truths. Sacrifice doesn't always feel like worship. I don't usually sing hymns when I'm awakened for the third time in one night. I don't usually think, *Wow, isn't motherhood beautiful?* when I'm wiping urine off the floor. But when we do these things as mothers, we *are* declaring something. We are declaring that the most beautiful life is the life poured out for others. In these actions, we imitate and therefore exalt Jesus who came to do lowly work among lowly people.

So, moms, I say to you, keep speaking the language of sacrifice. Keep giving. Keep serving. Keep worshiping. Let the God who gave you a view of mercy also give you a view of what matters most in his eternal kingdom. If your current perfume is Scent of Spit-up and if you have trouble putting together coherent sentences, know that you're not alone and it's not in vain. With every read of a board book or repeat of "The Wheels on the Bus," we may sound a little less like someone who used to talk about "encylopaedia as a form of moral enquiry" but more like Jesus. With every sleepless night or diaper explosion cleanup, we may look a little less like our young carefree selves but more like Jesus. The sacrifices of motherhood make us a little more like Jesus who showed us that the end of sacrifice is not ultimately loss but gain.

Reflection Questions

1) Make a list of the things Jesus gave up when He became man. Then list what he gained through that sacrifice. (You might check out Philippians 2:5–11 to help with this exercise.) In what ways do those gains have more value than what He sacrificed?

2) List some ways you sacrifice for your children. Then list some of what you gain through those sacrifices. In what ways do the gains have more value than what you sacrificed?

3) In Romans 12, Paul draws a direct connection between a) viewing God's mercy and b) sacrificing yourself and worshiping God. What are ways we can daily keep God's mercy in view and therefore honor God through the nitty-gritty sacrifices of motherhood?

4

Health and Hygiene

Lost Vitamins, Eye-Logs, and the Mirror of Motherhood

The moment you get that positive pregnancy test, you are a mom, and all moms want is to do give their children what's best in every way: healthy foods, regular baths, enough outdoor time, frequent stimulation of their brains. As a new mom, I was no exception. I definitely played my oldest classical music when our first son was a baby because I thought it would make him smarter. The other three are going to be below average, I guess, because they got about a thousand run-throughs of "Hot Dog!" from *Mickey Mouse Clubhouse* and exactly zero Bach.

When I first became a mother, I was overwhelmed with trying to keep my baby healthy. I remembered taking a general health and hygiene class in school, and then, in motherhood, I realized I was now also responsible for the health and hygiene of my children. With that first kid, though, I had the time and energy to do a lot of things I didn't have time or energy to do for my next few kids. I remember Young-Mom Emily with her one child, thinking she was stressed and tired. I laugh at Young-Mom Emily. I want to *be* Young-Mom Emily. Oh, the things I could get done and the naps I would take if I was Young-Mom Emily! But I digress. Life gets harder with each kid, which means that with each kid, you get a pass to lower your standards a little. This is an unwritten but official rule. I promise.

For example, for the first child, you will have bath time every other night religiously—maybe even every night if you're a real bath zealot. You will take lots of time to splash and play and sing little bath time songs. Bath time will be so special. When the second child comes, bath time will still be a priority, but it will become a little more stressful as you try to figure out how to manage two wet and slippery children at the same time. By the third child, you will look up on Saturday and realize none of your children have been bathed since Monday. Oops. When you do get around to bathing them, it will be all about efficiency. No time for play or bath songs. Rush those dirty little people through like an army drill sergeant. Soap. Rinse. Hand off to dad for towel-drying. Don't feel bad. They are *clean*.

For your first child, you may also have time to do things like make your own baby food and keep track of having your baby try a new food every three or four days. And you will make sure that *you* try all the food first. I am still making baby food for my fourth, mostly because they want to charge a dollar for a tiny jar of sweet potatoes. Highway robbery. But otherwise baby four is subsisting primarily on whatever is easiest to puree on the spot. Avocado for days. Just like bathtime, meals have become all about efficiency, people. I won't pretend that I don't have underlying feelings of guilt for not making him pureed kale like I did my oldest. Of course, I also felt guilty about feeding my oldest pureed kale because that flavor may be a form of cruel and unusual punishment. The point is, our first kid tried all kinds of different foods. Our fourth is fortunate to have mild variation in his diet.

No matter where you are on this spectrum—whether your children get a quick weekly bath or a balanced diet including pureed kale—if you've been a mom for more than five minutes, I would guess you're familiar with Mom Guilt. We want so desperately to do what's best for our kids, but we're afraid our best is going to fall short. So we feel guilty if we let our kids watch a little too much TV because we needed them to calm down for a while, or—worse yet—*we* needed to calm down for a while. We feel guilty if we feed them chicken nuggets and chips for the third day that week because we haven't managed to get to the store. We feel guilty if we don't bathe them every night because we are simply too tired. That mom on Instagram who seems to have it all together? We bet she would've bathed them and read stories to them for hours with joy.

Back in the day, before television and internet and social media, I think we would not have had so much mom guilt. Sure, moms then compared themselves with their neighbors and people they saw in magazines, but they didn't carry guilt around 24/7 in their pockets like I do. I remember my mom telling me how she could only breastfeed me for a few months: "I had three older kids, and they told me it was because of stress," she said, shrugging it off like it was no big deal. Today, however, we are all so connected that we constantly compare what we do to what others do. Today, women like my mom have to deal with countless Facebook articles and mommy Instagrammers subtly (or not so subtly) guilting her for her inadequate supply of "liquid gold." In the internet age, we are constantly assaulted with information on the ten million ways we can ruin our children.

It's exhausting.

Sometimes, we need to just take a step back, breathe, and rest in the sovereignty of God we thought about in chapter two. Your children won't be ruined if they watch an extra hour of TV because you are comatose on the couch after a long, sleepless night with the baby. They won't be ruined if they eat frozen pizza for lunch, which mine did this very day. That said, I'm not advocating for letting our kids watch endless TV or feeding them pizza every day. I'm not advocating for neglect or even mediocrity.

I am advocating for grace.

We absolutely need to do our best for our kids, but we also need to give ourselves grace when our best falls short of what *we think* our best should be. Who decides what is best? Who holds us accountable? It often feels like it's the whole world—every mommy Instagram account or Pinterest board—but it's just God. He knows our limits, our capacity, and what our best actually is on every day of our lives, just like He knows the number of hairs on our heads. Some days, we manage to clean the bathrooms, organize that random drawer full of expired coupons and loose screws, bake muffins, and spend quality time with each kid. Other days, we barely manage to keep them and ourselves alive and maybe cut a grand total of three fingernails. Some days, we thrive; other days, we just survive, and that's okay.

I will tell you that my children get those grace-laced chicken nuggets more than I'd like to admit. They've got protein right? But I also try to give them a gummy vitamin every morning. Balance. In fact, gummy vitamins and I go way back. We have a history.

When my oldest was about three-and-a-half years old, we were going through the "threenage" stage. I've never really liked the term, but alas, it describes a very real trial. They say the twos are terrible, but the threes with my son about did me in. I think the hardest part was spending all of my time with someone who had the reasoning capacity of a chimpanzee and the emotions of a menopausal woman. Whereas I once spent my days pondering things like the intricacies of St. Anselm's ontological argument, I now had to expend my intellectual energy trying to convince my son that all of his gummy vitamins were in fact the same size.

This brings us to what shall live in infamy as the Great Gummy Vitamin Debacle. I bought him gummy vitamins because he always wanted my prenatal ones. This was maybe the biggest mistake of my life. He carried his daily vitamin around and ate it in tiny bites until he inevitably lost whatever remained, at which point the world, of course, would end.

The world was ending for the fourth time in a single week one morning before we left for my weekly Bible study. He held onto the vitamin the whole ride there and was still guarding it when I dropped him off in childcare. He was uncharacteristically clingy that morning, so I had to pry myself away from his grasp and make a break for it. I figured he would calm down pretty quickly, but when I heard his wails from the other room, I decided to check on him. I came back to find him loudly lamenting the loss of his beloved vitamin. He was in hysterics, and I was about to lose it too. It had been a rough morning, and I had already lost my temper a few times, but now I had an audience.

I struggled to keep my cool. All I wanted was to go drink some coffee and talk to adults for a change. I was looking around for the vitamin when the childcare worker tapped my shoulder, hesitated, and then finally said to me, "You have a gummy on your butt." Yes, that's right. The gummy vitamin that he had slathered in saliva and carried around like Gollum's *Precious* had somehow become attached to my posterior, probably when he was clinging to me for dear life at the drop-off minutes earlier.

There I was, reaching behind me and trying to turn to look at my rear end like an idiot, but I still could not locate the accursed vitamin. So the childcare worker, who was at best an acquaintance, had to pull the gummy off my butt, which I then handed to my son because, well, why not? I'm sure I had let him eat worse than a butt vitamin. At least it came off of *my* backside. I walked back to my study group feeling exhausted and a little defeated. How had our morning turned into such a train wreck over something so silly? I guess "the best laid schemes of mice and men go oft awry" ... and the best intended gummy vitamins oft end up on our butts.

The point of all this is that this motherhood gig is hard. And not infrequently absurd. It doesn't always bring out the best in me. In fact, it often feels like it brings out the worst in me. Honestly, if we hadn't been at church during that gummy vitamin fit, I probably would have lost it with my son. I barely even kept my cool *at* church. Even though we try desperately to do our best for our kids, we inevitably come up short. Just as I was walking around unaware that I had a gooey, slobbery gummy vitamin nub on my pants that morning, I often walk around unaware of some of the ugliest things in my heart. And just as the gummy vitamin was eventually revealed, motherhood will eventually reveal ugly parts of ourselves.

Many people have said that parenting is one of the most sanctifying experiences. Let me tell you, it's true. The problem is that I once thought sanctification meant that I would become more and more holy by becoming more and more lovely, but there are many times in motherhood when I feel like I am becoming less holy because sanctification means revealing my sin and provoking repentance. I thought motherhood was going to make me softer, warmer, kinder, but as I move through the different stages of parenting, I sometimes feel like I am going the opposite direction. The subsequent mom guilt can be heavy. When I look back on the Great Gummy Vitamin Debacle, I hang my head. I replay the moments of my anger and frustration, my impatience and irritability, my harsh words that seemed to slip out uncontrollably, and I cringe.

But remembering that day makes me realize what I am learning about sanctification—that it can appear to get worse before it gets better. A glass of dirty water sitting still can look clear until it's shaken. Maybe your unbathed child appears clean enough until you get up close and take a whiff. So too with our hearts.

The uncomfortable truth is that I am far more like my children than I am unlike them. I am impatient with their impatience, angry with their anger, and annoyed when their selfishness gets in the way of my own. At times, I am tempted to justify my sin. *It's not my fault! I wouldn't be so irritable if my children weren't leaving banana peels in every room of the house. I wouldn't be so angry if I didn't have to deal with the fiftieth sibling squabble of the day. I didn't used to be impatient. I didn't used to be angry. My kids must have made me impatient and angry.*

But outward circumstances don't create sin in our hearts. They merely bring it to the surface. My children's behavior doesn't cause me to be more sinful. It exposes the sin that's already there.

The problem is not without but within. When I fail to recognize this, I am nothing more than a hypocrite, scolding my children for their shortcomings without first stopping to assess and confess my own. If I miss this, I will never see myself clearly, much less my children. If I'm going to help my children get the specks out of their eyes, I must first get the log out of mine.

The Log and the Speck

The metaphor of the log and the speck comes from the Sermon on the Mount (Matthew 5–7), where Jesus details what the Kingdom of Heaven is like. In chapter 7, He uses a metaphor to address the issue of hypocrisy:

> Why do you see the speck that is in your brother's eye, but do not notice the log that is in your own eye? Or how can you say to your brother, "Let me take the speck out of your eye," when there is the log in your own eye? You hypocrite, first take the log out of your own eye, and then you will see clearly to take the speck out of your brother's eye. (Matthew 7:3–5)

Jesus knew what we are all prone to do: fixate on the sin of others while being blind to our own sin. Our perception and judgment of others is skewed because our perception and judgment of ourselves is skewed. We fall into hypocrisy and self-righteous judgment because we magnify the flaws of others and minimize our own.

Jesus calls us to turn our fingers around, to quit pointing out what's wrong with other people, and first ask what is wrong with ourselves. Our own sin should always take first priority.

This is easy enough for me to explain, but much more difficult for me to live out. I've always thought of myself as a fairly gracious, easygoing person. I'm the youngest of four, and as they say about youngest children, I learned to go with the flow and to stay out of conflict. I was chill. But it turns out that was mostly because before I had my own kids, I didn't have many experiences that challenged my easygoing-ness. Now I have plenty. I did not feel particularly gracious when my son tried to hold in his poop forever and inevitably started to go in his underwear. Nor did I go with the flow when we went for a nice family dinner to celebrate my birthday, and my daughter whined and complained the whole time.

Whether through missed bath times or lost tempers, motherhood has a way of obliterating our high opinions of ourselves. It has a way of showing us our logs.

The Mirror of Motherhood

After thirty-six cumulative months of rent-free living in my body, my children all had the nerve to come out looking exactly like their dad. Apparently, my genes are placebo genes. In fact, our oldest looks so much like my husband it's a little unnerving, but in terms of personality, he is just like me, and let me tell you, it is not always flattering. *Was I this lazy and whiney as a kid?* (Answer: yes.) *Was I this selfish?* (Answer: yes.) *How did my mom handle it?* (Answer: Jesus and ice cream.)

I like to think I've come a long way from that whiney, selfish version of myself, but on some days, she is obviously alive and well. The only difference is that now, I'm the one needing Jesus and ice cream.

You see, motherhood is like a mirror. When He gives us children, God gives us a reflection of ourselves. As we look at our children's shortcomings, we will respond in wisdom or folly, sight or blindness. Proverbs 9:9 says, "Give instruction to a wise man, and he will be wiser still; teach a righteous man, and he will increase in learning." So too the wise mother. She gazes at the picture God provides of herself and adds to her wisdom. Rather than self-righteously blinding herself to her sin, she looks, sees, and adjusts her own assessment of herself. She looks at her children, their grumbling and complaining, their selfishness and folly, and she understands that that is exactly how she appears before God. She then knows exactly what her children need: the same grace, the same firm but tender correction that she herself needs.

Without God's intervention, we are blind to our sin, and because of our hypocrisy we are blind to our own blindness. We think we see clearly, but we don't. It takes the intervention of God to give us sight, but that intervention is not a one-time event. The gospel is like a set of corrective lenses we must pick up and put on every day. It restores our distorted perception of reality so that we can see ourselves as we really are.

God uses the sanctifying process of motherhood to remind us that though we are mothers who correct and admonish our children, we are also children who need to be corrected and admonished by Him.

As Paul Tripp writes in *Parenting*,

> Think about how beautiful this is. In every moment as you are parenting your children, the heavenly Father is parenting you. As you are lovingly confronting your children with the hope that they would confess their need and commit to change, the heavenly Father is confronting you. As you seek to encourage your children toward what is right, your Father in heaven is working to grow the desire in you. In all those moments when you intervene to protect your children from their own foolish choices, the great Father is protecting you from you.[4]

Even as we try to do our best to raise our kids and teach them the gospel, we must not forget that we still desperately need it ourselves. We may have grasped its information, but its transformative power is still at work in us. *We* are sinful children. *We* need Jesus to give us new hearts. In God's kindness and wisdom as a Father—as a good parent—He uses the brokenness and neediness of our children to reveal those same things in us.

---

4. Paul Tripp, *Parenting: 14 Gospel Principles That Can Radically Change Your Family* (Wheaton, IL: Crossway, 2016), 41.

Handling Their Specks

How we respond to the mirror God provides will directly affect our parenting. How we deal with our "logs" will determine how we deal with our children's "specks." If we're not careful, we will all be like the fool battering our children with the log of our self-righteousness. So how *can* we help our children see their sin? How can we address the speck in their eye without making ourselves into the hypocrites whom Jesus spoke of? In his book *Studies in the Sermon on the Mount,* D. Martin-Lloyd Jones perfectly addressed these questions. He wrote,

> You are going to handle a soul, you are going to touch the most sensitive thing in man. How can we get the little mote out? There is only one thing that matters at that point, and that is that you should be humble, you should be sympathetic, you should be so conscious of your own sin and your own unworthiness, that when you find it in another, far from condemning you feel like weeping. You are full of sympathy and compassion; you really do want to help. You have so enjoyed getting rid of the thing in yourself that you want him to have the same pleasure and the same joy. You cannot be a spiritual oculist until you yourself have clear sight.[5]

5. D. Martyn Lloyd-Jones, *Studies in the Sermon on the Mount* (Grand Rapids, MI: Eerdmans, 1997), 2:181.

I have a vivid memory from my childhood. I had snuck into my neighbor's backyard while they were out of town and was caught jumping on their trampoline and eating popcorn with a friend. Clearly, I was headed down a path of destruction. Okay, maybe it wasn't that bad, but I was a consummate rule-follower, and I felt riddled with guilt. My mother sent me to my room where I was left trembling in my boots to await my father. When he came home, he did not get angry. He did not even wag his finger at me. Rather, he told me a story from his own childhood when he had gotten in big trouble for pouring sunscreen into his neighbor's pool.

I remember that experience so well because what my father showed me was empathy and grace. He didn't excuse what I had done or tell me it was no big deal, but he identified with me in my sin. He showed me that he was not so different from me. He handled my speck with care.

When I correct my children, I hope to give them a taste of that. I try to show them my own humanity. I tell them, "Mommy gets angry sometimes too," and when I do, they're probably thinking, *Yeah, we know.* Or I try to tell them my own stories about how God has changed my heart. And when I fail, I try to be faithful to confess and ask their forgiveness. The Lord knows I don't do this perfectly, but I hope they look back and remember moments like I remember with my dad.

Hypocritical, condescending parenting will never endear our children to us or to Jesus. More likely, it will drive them away. A lifestyle of brokenness, contrition, confession, and repentance will win their souls. The message should not be that we look down on them from the lofty heights of our own righteousness but that we are with them in the muck and mire of sin. Our responses should convey that God in His mercy has reached down to pull us out right alongside them, and it is He and He alone who renews our hearts and minds. We are His messenger, through word and deed, of love to our children. The picture we give them is undoubtedly marred, but in the day-to-day sacrificing and serving of motherhood, God is refining and clarifying and sharpening His image in us so that it might be better reflected to these little ones.

A Two-Way Mirror

Thankfully, God is in the business of restoring broken vessels like moms into means of grace. If motherhood is a mirror, it is a two-way mirror. Through our children, God gives us a picture of what we are really like. And through us, though our kids don't even know it yet, He is daily giving *them* a picture of what He is like. When we handle their specks with compassion and care as my father did for me, we give them a glimpse of who God the Father is.

Not only is God using the work of parenting to

reflect His love to our children, He is using it to magnify it for us. Just like our children, we too are works in progress. We're all kind of a hot mess walking around in need of a bath. We might also get grumpy when we need a nap. We also don't like it when we don't get our way or when we must wait for things we want. We also lose our minds over our lost gummy vitamins. And when we do, God does what a good father does: He loves us anyway.

While we often fall short as mothers even when we give our best, our heavenly Father never does. Our need never exhausts him. Our brokenness never repels Him. Rather, our insufficiency evokes His compassion and mobilizes His grace. "He knows our frame; He remembers that we are dust" (Psalm 103:14). Jesus invites us to lay the mom guilt aside and come—butt vitamins, logs, and all. We are His children, and He will handle our specks with care. He will meet us with His love.

Reflection Questions

1) How do your children serve as mirrors for you? What "logs" has the mirror of motherhood exposed in your life? How does the gospel make this exposure of sin a hopeful experience?

2) How does the gospel free us from the cycle of mom guilt? Read 1 John 1:7–9 and think about what you say

to someone struggling with mom guilt. Now, tell that to yourself.

3) Each child has his or her own unique set of weaknesses and "specks." Write down specific ways you can handle more carefully the specks you see in your own children.

5

Phys Ed

Maternal Olympics, Hitting Our Limits, Finding True Strength

Once upon a time, I was what you would call an athlete. I am the youngest of four girls, and while my father longed for a son with whom he could play ball, I was the closest he got. With reasonable physical agility and an ability to run long distances in short times, I passed for a decent soccer player and cross country runner in high school. I look back at those days with a mixture of awe and confusion now. How was I ever in that good of shape? My current self can barely comprehend how my past self managed to run five miles a day in the Oklahoma heat because my current self now gets a little winded going up the stairs while holding a basket of clean laundry in my air-conditioned home. Besides a brief stint with indoor soccer after my oldest was born, my days of such fitness and athleticism are long gone. I'm at the place in life now where I consider a nice, slow walk good exercise.

However, just because I am not an athlete in the

traditional sense anymore does not mean I am not an athlete. Whether you were a star forward or you flunked P. E. in high school, when you become a mom, you become an athlete. The sports look a little different than they did then, but they are no less intense and require just as much grit and tenacity, if not more.

Motherhood Sporting Events

Maybe like me, after having kids, you don't have much time or energy to go to the gym, and you wonder how you'll keep your strength up. Do not worry. You will still get your workouts in because there are a few things in motherhood that I have decided should be Olympic sports. Most of them involve toddlers. First up: toddler teeth brushing.

From about six months to two years old, toddlers grow a mouthful of teeth, and for some reason, around twelve months, they decide to strongly object to having them brushed. Either that or they only want to wrench the toothbrush from your hands so they can suck on it like a lollipop. While this might make them happy, it proves largely ineffective in achieving the actual goal of clean baby teeth. Thus, you will need to prepare yourself for a showdown every morning and night.

After three toddlers, I have almost perfected this sport. At first, my son would squirm and escape down the hallway while I chased after him, wielding a toothbrush and lectures about cavities, but after a few months of practicing training maneuvers, I was able to keep him in the bathroom. I've become adept at pinning a child, clamping two tiny arms under one of mine while quickly brushing that child's teeth with the other. My best time is twenty seconds, and I'm hoping to take the gold in this event in the next summer Olympics.

This takes us to one of the oldest Olympic sports: wrestling. Motherhood puts a spin on this classic with *diaper* wrestling. This takes a lot of the same strength and agility as the teeth-brushing, but it is more challenging because you may at any moment be sprayed with bodily fluids. Again for some reason, at about nine months, babies decide that having their diaper changed is torture of the highest degree. It's like wrestling an alligator into a diaper. I do not remember having my own diaper changed, but I gather from my children that there is nothing worse in all of the world—save, perhaps, having their faces wiped. All I know is that instead of playing soccer for thirteen years, I should have been practicing my wrestling moves. Soccer gave me incredible leg strength but essentially left me with the arms of a T-rex.

You might think that a twenty-pound infant would be no match for a grown, adult woman, but you would be wrong. I remember how my oldest would summon all of his angry baby strength to battle me as I cruelly tried to remove his bodily waste from his pants and give him a fresh, clean diaper.

Currently, I am being outmatched in this sport by my youngest son. I can only compete in it as a team: my husband holds down his arms while I manage the legs and hind quarters. Luckily for me, my husband works from home, so I rarely need to go it alone. When I do, I barely escape poop disaster. At the end of our regular wrestling matches, I am quite literally out of breath, so you can bet I count it as working out.

Lastly, the Toddler Olympics include a rodeo-style event. I grew up in Oklahoma, which means I have attended my fair share of rodeos. I am by no means a rodeo fan, but I am familiar with bulldogging, or steer wrestling, in which the cowboy launches himself from his horse onto a running bull in order to wrestle it to the ground. The cowboy must use both speed and precision to keep up with the bull and land in the perfect position to tame it. If he jumps too late or too soon, he will miss, and the steer will escape. Timing is everything. Once he lands, he must wrap his arms around the horns and twist the stubborn beast to the ground. The task is not complete until the steer is down and all of its feet are pointing to one side.

Now, I am no cowgirl, and my toddler is thankfully no horned steer, but I can tell you that when that little person breaks away, I feel like a professional bulldogging queen. Is he running away with an open container of diaper cream? Not today. Is he heading for the stairs at church or for a display of breakables at the department store? I'll put a stop to that in under five seconds.

So break out your cowgirl hats, Mommas. You might not be as strong and agile as you were in your glory days, but you may yet outrun your toddler ... even though those little legs can move surprisingly fast. Extra points for difficulty if you manage to do this while wearing a baby or while thirty-eight weeks pregnant. Of course, no one will be handing us ribbons when we single-handedly save our children from causing disaster, but we will sure feel like we deserve one, or at least a bowl of ice cream after bedtime.

Weakness Exposed

The glory days of youthful athleticism may be behind us, but motherhood will still take a lot of strength—in more than one sense of the word. It certainly taxes us physically. We have to grow the baby. Birth the baby. Feed the baby. And then when the baby becomes mobile, we have to keep the baby from his or her untimely ending. This side of thirty I'm starting to feel it. I can still chase down my two-year-old, but by the time I've nabbed him, I feel like I need a little oxygen. At the end of my last pregnancy, I had to run about forty yards to chase down my son. We were walking around a middle school track near our house and he made a breakaway for the street. The next day, I was thankful for his safety but legitimately and embarrassingly sore. It's a lot on our bodies ... and it's a lot on our souls too. For motherhood not only reveals our physical weakness. It reveals our spiritual weakness as well.

I felt this keenly when my daughter was around two years old. It was such a rough stage with her. She was very emotional and also very obsessed with me. I couldn't leave the room without her freaking out. If I locked the door so I could shower without an audience, she would stand outside the door and wail, even though her dad was literally standing there next to her. We pretty much lived in meltdown city. Putting her to bed became a nightmare. One of my favorite comedians, Jim Gaffigan, likens putting kids to bed as a reverse hostage situation in which the parents plead with the children to just stay in their rooms, and after living through this stage with my daughter, I'd say that's pretty accurate. By eight o'clock, I was willing to do almost anything to get her locked—I mean, tucked—away in her room for bed.

That same year, I remember one night in particular that could probably make the highlight reel for my top five worst mom moments. My daughter had fallen outside shortly before bed and scraped her knee on the sidewalk. I coddled appropriately, cleaned it up, and then started the bedtime process because it was a scraped knee, not a lost limb, and this tired momma was desperate for some quiet, kid-free time. My daughter, however, acted like she had been gravely wounded in battle. She refused to wear pajamas that might possibly come within five inches of her boo-boo. She insisted instead on wearing a six-to-twelve-month-sized Wonder Woman costume with a skirt which, being about four sizes too small, would come nowhere near her minor flesh wound. I threw up my hands in frustration and wondered how my life had become this ridiculous but decided to cave and let her wear the absurdly small costume to bed. I had given her exactly what she wanted, and yet still she continued to melt down over her itty bitty scrape while my patience continued to wane. After what felt like eons of trying to calm her down and coax her to bed, I snapped. There I was facing off with this tiny, little, slightly crazy person in a too-small Wonder Woman costume. I *lost* it.

I don't mean I raised my voice a little. No, I raged at my daughter. I'm pretty sure I even said a few choice words that definitely would not make the cut in a children's movie.

It was not pretty. My supply of maternal patience and grace and long-suffering turned out to be insufficiently small. I felt completely empty. I had nothing left to give, not a single ounce of energy or willpower to mother the Wonder Woman situation with any semblance of grace.

Eventually my daughter cried herself to sleep and I retreated to my room swimming in a sense of guilt and failure.

I had been put to the pajama drama test and failed miserably.

The Lie of Self-Empowerment

In today's world, we hear a lot about the power within us, particularly for women. We're obsessed with asserting our strength and indestructibility. *I am woman, hear me roar.* Self-actualization is the gospel of our day. We just need to tap into our inner strength. Think positive thoughts, and then positive things will manifest in our lives. All that we need for strength and happiness is within.

What attractive lies.

Even in Christian circles, we can dress this up with a little religious language and call it truth: *God wants you to discover your own strength. God wants you to stop holding yourself back. God wants to unlock your potential. God has a special plan for special little you.* We can treat God like a magic genie that puts us on center stage.

Ironically, what should encourage us can end up sounding incredibly discouraging. How do these words hit a mother struggling with postpartum depression? Or a woman dealing with chronic pain? How crippling it is to hear, "Just do better," or "Unlock your hidden strength," when she simply cannot do better and has not one ounce of strength left after a sleepless night or a showdown with her irrational toddler?

The darkest days of my motherhood journey came a few months after my third child was born. He had been sleeping well for the first three months, and then suddenly he wasn't. To top it off, my two-year old decided to throw herself out of her bed screaming multiple times a night. My nights were a horror, which meant my days were marked by exhaustion and fraught with short tempers. I became depressed and anxious. How could I do this job with no sleep? How could I carry on? Would it ever get better? It honestly felt like it wouldn't. I remember coming across a quote on Instagram that said, "True power is living the realization that you are your own healer, hero, and leader." When I read that, I scoffed cynically and then sighed because in those months, I sure didn't feel like any of those things. I couldn't see a light at the end of the tunnel, and I didn't need to be told to find the power within because I had no power inside of myself. I needed to be told to find the power *outside* of myself.

Sometimes it seems our culture has made God out to be someone who comes along just to help us realize our own greatness. In actuality, the God of the Bible has no interest in nurturing the delusion of our inner power and strength. The woman who trusts in herself? The one who depends on her own strength? The lie calls her empowered, but God calls her *cursed*. The lie promises she'll be a flourishing tree, but God tells her she will be like a shriveled bush.

> Cursed is the one who trusts in man, who draws strength from mere flesh and whose heart turns away from the LORD. That person will be like a bush in the wastelands; they will not see prosperity when it comes. They will dwell in the parched places of the desert, in a salt land where no one lives (Jeremiah 17:5-6, NIV).

Talk about some harsh imagery.

During some days or even seasons of motherhood, we may feel like that bush. The world tells us we're enough, but we will often feel that we're never enough and that we never have enough. Not enough patience. Not enough grace. Not enough energy. We will feel dried up and spent and buckling under the weight of our children's relentless neediness. That's how I felt in those difficult days when my children decided to boycott sleep, and I still regularly have days where I feel the same way, even though they all now sleep through the night.

Have you ever considered how fragile and limited we are? We considered some of our limitations during our physics lesson, but there are plenty more to name. Our bodies require food every few hours to keep working. We may last days without completely shutting down, but go long enough without nutrition and our bodies will die. We also require sleep simply to function. Every night, we essentially turn ourselves off to recharge. In fact, sleep deprivation has sometimes been used as a form of torture. Sounds effective to me: I'm pretty sure that I would spill national secrets after a few days of no sleep. But motherhood gives you a small taste of that kind of agonizing fatigue. In designing us such that we need food and sleep, God gives us daily reminders of what we really are. Dust. A mist that appears for a while and then vanishes. We are not the mighty beings we imagine ourselves to be. We are all too vulnerable.

Just as God intentionally reminds us of our physical limitations, He also intentionally reminds us of our spiritual weaknesses, and they often go together. During our sleep crisis, my patience and gracious attitude became essentially nonexistent. I'd yell at my kids for the crumbs all over the floor or the toothpaste all over the counter, and I'd huff and puff while cleaning up. Then came the inevitable feelings of guilt and failure followed by a futile resolve that I would do better by sheer force of will. *I will be a better mom. I will!* But then we'd have a rough night, and I would struggle to tap into my inner joy that had shrunken down to the size of a raisin long ago dropped into the dark recesses of the couch. I was frustrated with myself and with God. Why wouldn't He answer my prayers to make my children sleep so that I could be a better mom? Did He *want* me to ruin them?

I kept trying to scrape together my strength, but God kept pressing on my weakness. He kept wounding my pride. God will continue bringing us to the edge of ourselves and even push us over it, but if we can trust wounds from a friend, surely we can hold dear those from our God (Proverbs 27:6). He is too kind to puff us up, and too good to let us believe that we have what it takes. Contrary to what the lie will tell us, God's purpose for our lives isn't to build our self-confidence. It is to destroy it. This is not ultimately to tear us down, but to rebuild us on something better. He will deconstruct the façade of our passing strength so that He can reconstruct a deep reliance on His enduring strength. And He will use motherhood to do it.

Everything the world promises God flips on its head. We cannot get to life without going through our death. We cannot get to glory without going through our humility. We cannot get to true strength without going through our weakness. The world tells us that weakness is shameful, something to be overcome, but God tells us it is something to be embraced because the strength He offers is so much greater than the greatest strength we could muster ourselves. It is not the strong in spirit who are blessed, but the weak, the needy, the poor (Matthew 5:3).

We read earlier that we are cursed when we trust in ourselves or other people rather than the Lord, but that same passage in Jeremiah goes on to describe those who are blessed:

> But blessed is the one who trusts in the Lord, whose confidence is in him. They will be like a tree planted by the water that sends out its roots by the stream. It does not fear when heat comes; its leaves are always green. It has no worries in a year of drought and never fails to bear fruit." (Jeremiah 17:7–8, NIV)

I have often prayed this verse over my children. I long to see them be like that tree, deeply rooted and thriving, drinking from the streams of God and bearing much fruit, yet I forget to be like it myself. How often I feel more like that bush, dry and withered, barely hanging on in the wind. How often I try to put down roots into the thin and deficient soil of my own strength and righteousness. I am prone to wander in salty places and neglect the stream of living water.

Motherhood will bring the best of us to the brink of our physical and spiritual strength. It will show us how shallow the well of our patience and self-control and peace and graciousness is. Even exalted, fabled, maternal love will falter. Even the best kind of earthly motherhood has its limits. It is weak. But in the hands of our God, all of that weakness is transformed into beauty and power. Why? Because it leads us to a well of living water whose depths we cannot plumb, a love with limits we can never reach. Our weakness as mothers pushes us toward the One who, unlike us, lacks nothing—One whose strength is never depleted by the neediness of His children but is instead magnified by it.

We don't have what it takes for motherhood. Not even close. But our God does. So, let us live by that well. Let us plant ourselves by that stream and send our roots deep. Blessed is the one, blessed is the *mother*, who does this.

Reflection Questions

1) When have you encountered the lie of self-empowerment? How did it impact your thinking? How does it still? What made you realize that this lie wasn't delivering on its promise?

2) When have your physical and/or spiritual limitations as a mother brought you to the end of yourself? How did God's kindness meet you right in the midst of your weakness?

3) Jeremiah 17 contrasts the image of a dried up bush with a flourishing tree, but note that the difference is not in the plants themselves but in their *sources*. What thoughts and habits lead you to try to live out of your own strength? What thoughts and habits can you cultivate to root yourself by the streams of God?

6

Fashion

The Mom Uniform, Faulty Fig Leaves, the Better Covering of Christ

I may not be proud of this, but a big chunk of my summers in middle school was spent binge-watching episodes of What Not to Wear—before binge-watching was even a term.

In the show, family members or friends would nominate someone they knew who had terrible fashion. The (un)lucky winner would have to watch secret footage of themselves looking like a homeless person at the grocery store or the movies before they had to trash their entire wardrobe and purchase a new one, following rules set by fashion gurus Clinton and Stacy.

There were usually two kinds of people selected for this show: eccentric people who had weird fashion sense and frumpy people who put little time or money into their wardrobes. The latter group was often middle-aged mothers. Oh, how I judged them! How could they let themselves go like that? Didn't they care? I was sure I would never end up like that. I think my sisters and I even made some kind of pact.

But it is not unusual these days for me to run to the grocery store, glance in the car mirror, and think I look like a contestant from *What Not to Wear*. The Proverbs say pride goes before a fall ... in this case, a fashion fall.

I know now what I didn't know then about those mothers on *What Not to Wear*. Those women looked the way they did at 45 because at about 25 or 30 they started having babies, and from then on they spent around ninety percent of their time and energy raising those babies and the other ten percent showering whenever they could. They wore whatever was cleanest at the moment and lacked stylish clothes, at least partly because babies don't care about fashion. And because shopping *with* children is basically a nightmare, while shopping *without* them is nearly impossible, especially if you have a nursing baby who won't take a bottle (like one of my children who shall remain nameless).

Last summer, I looked in my closet and realized about half of my summer clothes were from college and the other half were maternity pieces. *How did this happen?* I wondered. *How do I have basically no up-to-date clothes? And how am I going to jump back into fashion since I stopped paying attention when skinny jeans and infinity scarves were still the thing and now find myself in a land of crop tops and mom jeans? Is it 2022 or 1999? How does one just start wearing overalls again? I wish I still had my jean jacket from ninth grade.*

I was once a fashionable person, though dressing myself got off to a rocky start. In second grade, my mom let me start picking out my clothes. What did I choose? Sweatpants and a giant t-shirt with my older sister's basketball jersey over it. It came down to my knees, and I thought I was the coolest tomboy ever. Mary-Kate Olsen from *It Takes Two* was my fashion goddess. In third grade, I continued my tomboy look, pairing a backwards hat with my favorite t-shirt that said "You play with dolls. I play soccer." Looking back, this sounded a little condescending as well as a little dishonest since I did also, in fact, play with dolls. But my crush once paid me a compliment on this shirt, so I began wearing it weekly. By fourth grade, I had arrived. I remember the Christmas when I was ten: I got new JNCO jeans, a blue knit shirt with stripes on the sleeves (because we were into weird stripes in the 90s), and a pair of blue glasses (think Elton John). I have a photo of me in this ensemble holding my new Walkman like I was posing for a *Limited Too* cover spread.

We shall not discuss the dark years of middle school. May the butterfly clip hair trend rest in peace. But by about age sixteen, I found my fashion groove.

I had a job and money to spend on things like cute clothes, and I did not have necessary expenses like diapers or electric bills. I had an excess of time to agonize over the perfect outfit and to curl my hair. I laugh now when I think about how much time I spent getting ready pre-kids.

Nowadays, I think jeans are fancy, and makeup is for church ... or other occasions where I might see people I know. If I'm going someplace where I won't know anyone, I look like a prime target for *What Not to Wear*. I'm not sure what that says about me, but it's probably something tremendously superficial.

Here's what I've concluded. There are two types of moms: moms who get dressed and do their makeup every day and moms who don't. If you are part of the former, more power to you. I sometimes wish I could be like you, but it sounds too exhausting. If, like me, you fall into the latter group, let me tell you what you need for your mom uniform.

The most important part of the mom uniform is stretchy pants. Call them yoga pants, leggings, sweats—whatever you want. Basically, you need pants that feel like pajamas and look like you're going to work out even though you are definitely not going to work out. Throw on a t-shirt, put your hair in a messy bun, and you're good to go for the day.

Gone are the days of searching for the perfect outfit. Here are the days of hoping you find the time to shower and brush your teeth. Because with all the balls in the air, it doesn't always happen. My daughter recently said to me, "Mommy, I look pretty more than you." Maybe it's time for a talk about vanity … and tact. But the truth is, she's kind of right. I don't have much time to worry about the way I look. And most of the time, I'm okay with it, though I won't pretend there aren't days when I wonder, *What happened to me?* Because sometimes I look at pictures of myself from college in a cute outfit with glowing skin, and it almost seems like I'm staring at an entirely different person.

Motherhood can be so consuming that we lose ourselves in it. Maybe we lose the things that once seemed to define us—looking fashionable, a job, a hobby. There are, after all, many things besides clothes that we "put on" in an attempt to shape who we want to be.

Ultimately, we're all looking for an identity. Maybe it begins with being the tomboy soccer player in an oversized basketball jersey or the JNCO jeans. Maybe then you quit soccer to pick up the violin. Some work at being the beautiful fashionista with perfect hair; others search for meaning in running for class president or being the valedictorian.

Adulthood isn't so different. We've just upped the stakes a little. Perfect grades have been traded for the perfect career. The class president is now a successful lawyer. That girl with the best clothes and hair that somehow always looked perfect ... well, she may still have the best clothes, and her hair may still somehow looks perfect. Is it magic? I think so. Only now, maybe she has perfect little mini-me children as well. I guess the perfect hair of the mother will be visited upon the hair of the daughter to the third and fourth generations.

Whether it's great fashion sense or great achievement, we're all looking for something within ourselves to define us and set us apart. This is not a new thing. This is the human condition, and it started all the way back in the beginning with Adam and Eve who also had a great fashion fall.

Paradise Lost, Identity Lost

Before sin came along, Adam and Eve had a secure identity, and that identity depended on their unbroken relationship with their Creator. They, the Bible says, "were both naked and were not ashamed" (Genesis 2:25). This was both literally and spiritually true. Untouched by sin, they had nothing to hide, nothing to fear. They needed nothing extra to make themselves presentable.

Then, the serpent whispered, "You can be like God without God. You can be enough without Him." Believing this lie, they chose to disobey God and sought to define—or identify—themselves apart from Him. It is only then that they realized they were naked. It is only then that they were ashamed. It is only then they felt their inadequacies and tried to hide from God and from each other. In desperation, they used fig leaves to cover themselves. Only after the fall—after they chose to seek an identity based within themselves and not in their God—did they shatter their God-given identity.

Now, I'm not that familiar with fig leaves, but I imagine they didn't do the job very well. There are no leaf garments walking the runway these days, and that is surely for good reason. Because even if leaves could have covered their shame, they wouldn't have lasted long. They would soon wither and fade. Any identity we make for ourselves apart from God is exactly like that: impermanent and ultimately insufficient. God knew those leaves wouldn't cut it, so He gave them the durable skins of an animal to wear instead—the first sacrifice for sin. And just as He offered Adam and Eve something more lasting than fig leaves, He offers us an identity that will last longer than anything we can come up with on our own. To receive it, we must first lay down our fig leaves.

My journey to letting go of my fig leaves began in college. At that time, my identity was irrevocably wrapped up in my academic success. This became all too apparent my sophomore year of college. For some inexplicable reason, I decided to pretend to be a morning person and sign up for early classes. I also took over a full load of courses, including the dreaded physics. All of this led to the end of my 4.0 GPA. I remember going on a walk and crying, basically questioning my entire existence.

I promise I'm not normally that dramatic, and let me tell you, my standards for myself have fallen dramatically since then (see the aforementioned Great Gummy Vitamin Debacle). But at the time, my despair at my "ruined" GPA was over the top because it wasn't simply about grades. It was about who I thought I was. I had to learn that my identity and worth were not ultimately determined by my grades, but by Jesus. Now in my early thirties and well out of college, I am still learning the same lesson—only now I am learning it as a mom. Maintaining a 4.0 in college is not what I would call easy, but I can tell you it is a breeze compared to trying to maintain a 4.0 in motherhood.

I am still learning not to find my identity in fig leaves. I must often remind myself that my identity cannot be found in how well my children behaved today. My identity cannot be found in how well *I* behaved today. My identity cannot be found in how quickly my body bounced back after pregnancy. My identity cannot be found in how clean my house is or in how organized my Tupperware drawer is. Praise the Lord for that. My identity can only be found in Jesus.

Say it with me: "My identity is in Jesus."

The Better Portion

Most of us are familiar with the story of Mary and Martha. If you are not, you can find it in Luke 10. Jesus comes to visit two sisters: Martha is busy serving and trying to be a good hostess, and she gets upset that Mary isn't helping, but is instead sitting at Jesus's feet, listening to him. For most of my life, I couldn't relate much to Martha, mostly because I much prefer sitting around to doing housework. Hosting people kind of stresses me out, though if my pastor came to visit, I think I'd at least remember to offer him a drink as opposed to sitting there doing nothing. But the truth is, Mary wasn't doing nothing. She was, according to Jesus, doing the most important thing.

Now, as a mom, I think I understand Martha a little better. Maybe Martha was letting her performance as a hostess and as a woman—her fig leaves, if you will—define her. Maybe Martha was so busy trying to please Jesus that she was too busy to know Jesus. Maybe Martha was so upset because her identity was tied up in the striving and the achieving and the image-maintaining. I think Jesus saw that. "Martha, Martha," he said, "you are anxious and troubled about many things, but one thing is necessary. Mary has chosen the good portion, which will not be taken away from her" (Luke 10:41).

Which portion do our children see us striving for? When we are old and dead and gone, what will they remember us by? Will they remember us as stressed and frantically striving for more fig leaves even as they withered in our hands? Or will they remember that we rested in the fact that we were covered by something better? Do we want them to learn that their worth is in their performance and image or that their worth is in Christ? If we want them to choose the good portion, we should also choose it for ourselves.

The Myth of the Perfect Mom

As moms, we feel a lot of pressure to do it all and have it all. Some days, it can feel like I am in competition with some kind of ideal mother and homemaker. Her house is always spotless and looks like a Pinterest board. She knows exactly how to fold a fitted sheet. She never loses her temper. She always has freshly baked cookies, and she has time to do creative, thrifty things like turn old pillowcases into adorable outfits. And she looks fabulous while doing it. Have you met her? I know you have. She lives in your head just like she lives in mine. (I call her Vicky because that sounds like someone who has her act annoyingly together.) Perhaps like me, you are tempted to work and strive to try to be your own personal Vicky. Perhaps like me, you have a gnawing sense of failure because, as it turns out, being Vicky is impossible.

(Sorry to all the Vickys out there. Nothing personal. You do you.)

When we try to find our worth in motherhood, we will always be striving, yet always coming up short. It is all as Solomon says, "striving after wind" (Ecclesiastes 1:14). And even if we do by some miracle, manage to have the perfect day, get the whole house clean, never sin once, knit a sweater, and teach our children a question from the catechism, we know we will not be able to do that all the time. Ultimately, anything we seek to build our identity on besides Jesus—even something good like being a good mom or a good homemaker—is like fig leaves: inadequate, fragile, and fleeting. Like Adam and Eve, we need God to provide something better to cover our inadequacies. We need Jesus.

God Does Not Need Us

Even though we may know in our minds that we need Jesus, we can still have this feeling that we need to be perfect. We may even think that God expects or needs us to be perfect! But this flows from a faulty understanding of God. God is completely self-sufficient. He is all powerful. He lacks nothing, "nor is He served by human hands, as though he needed anything, since He himself gives to all mankind life and breath and everything" (Acts 17:25).

God could have our house perfectly cleaned up in an instant (maybe I should start laying hands on my laundry and hoping for a miracle). He could have *us* perfectly cleaned up in an instant. He can and will be the One to ensure our children's salvation if that is His will. He doesn't need a single thing from us to accomplish His purposes. He chooses to make us part of His plan not because He needs us *but because we need Him.*

I remember a day when my oldest son was about three and my daughter was one, and motherhood was really starting to get hard. I would get so frustrated by the ridiculous things my son would cry about, and I would lose my temper multiple times a day. I was miserably failing to be Vicky. By the end of the day as I put my son to bed, I was exhausted and frustrated with my failure. Yet somehow, God turned it into the sweetest moment. I read my son a book that told the story of the gospel. While we read, God used the words to minister to me, and I cried softly into my son's freshly cleaned curls. As we talked about how Mommy sins, how Daddy sins, and how Jesus takes all our yucky sin, I could tell it started to mean something to my son because he could see that it meant something to me.

You see, if we're not careful, we can offer our kids the gospel but refuse it for ourselves. We can preach grace but live out legalism. In the end, it won't be our efforts at perfection that will lead our children to Jesus. It won't be the different identities we attempt to put on. If anything, these faulty attempts will only push them further away. The best way to show our children God's irresistible grace is to refuse to resist it ourselves, letting it fill all our broken places and spill over onto our kids.

It turns out that God's will for us is not to strive and strive and then sit in shame and self-pity when we fall short. He sees us running around in our mom uniforms, desperately trying to find our identities and worth in fleeting things, and His compassion moves Him to cover our shame. He knows our fig leaves aren't going to cut it. He provided real, substantial clothing to Adam and Eve, and He has provided us with something even better: a perfect identity given to us through the blood of Jesus. It's a revolutionary thought isn't it? When he looks at us, He doesn't see our dirty floors or our bad attitudes or our lost tempers. He sees the perfect righteousness of Christ. We are justified, Romans 5 tells us—justified by faith. We are saved, Ephesians 2 says—saved by grace. These are not personal achievements but gifts from God. We need to marinate our souls in these beautiful truths every single day.

In Christ, we can be spiritually naked, yet unashamed. God is not waiting for us to get our acts together so that He can use us as mothers. He doesn't need our fig leaves. He doesn't need our attempts to be perfect. He's got perfection on lock. What He *wants* is for us to get our messy, broken, sleep-deprived, possibly un-showered selves to the cross ... and He wants us to bring our children with us.

Reflection Questions

1) Make a list of specific roles or tasks (your own fig leaves) in which you are tempted to find your identity or earn God's approval. How have these fig leaves proven insufficient? How have they let you down?

2) Do you relate to Martha's busyness? Are you sometimes so busy trying to please Jesus that you forget to really know Jesus? How does the gospel free us from this striving?

3) How should the truth that God does not need anything from us influence our lives as mothers? How should this truth affect our relationship with Him? How might remembering your identity in Christ allow you to approach your daily tasks differently?

7
Chemistry

Becoming the Nucleus, Fighting Entropy, Searching for Lasting Peace

In college, I started out in the chemistry-heavy microbiology program because I loved—and I mean *loved*—chemistry in high school. I still have a glow-in-the-dark periodic table t-shirt. My friends and I had chemistry sleepovers to study for tests.

No, I actually wasn't part of the popular crowd. Why do you ask?

Think back with me now on chemistry class and you may recall experiments gone fabulously awry. If that's not motherhood, I do not know what is. And just as there are laws of chemistry we need to understand, there are also laws of motherhood.

The First Law of Mom-odynamics: You are the Nucleus

In chemistry, the first thing you learn about is the atom—the tiny entity, invisible to the naked eye, that makes up all matter. Atoms have a positively charged nucleus at the center and negatively charged electrons that exist in clouds around the nucleus. What on earth does this have to do with motherhood? Well, when you are a mom, *you* are the nucleus of your own little atomic family.

I am a textbook introvert, so sometimes while my children are miraculously playing well together, I will try to sneak away to my room to get time to myself. Within minutes—sometimes within seconds—the children appear at my side. It's like they need to be within a certain physical distance of me at all times. I am the center of their tiny universe, and they are always flitting about me. I don't even know why they like me so much. I am seriously not that much fun. But this is how motherhood works.

You are the nucleus, my friend, and your children are the electrons. They are drawn to you with magnetic force. (Okay, now we're mixing metaphors as well as fields of scientific study, but you get what I'm saying.) When you're a mom, there is no such thing as personal space. There is no bubble. That bubble was popped the moment that first human came screaming into your world. Wherever you go, they go. It's a law of the universe that we cannot fight. Accept it. Embrace it.

It won't last forever.

The Second Law of Mom-odynamics: Entropy

There is another important concept I learned about in chemistry: entropy. You may think you don't know what entropy is, but if you're a mom, you definitely know what it feels like. Basically, *entropy* is a fancy word for chaos or disorder. The screaming hot molecules of water vapor escaping from your tea kettle have greater entropy than the ordered, structured molecules of frozen water. And the second law of thermodynamics says that in an isolated system, entropy will always increase over time. In other words, things in the universe naturally tend toward chaos and disorder.

This is true in motherhood too. As moms, we invest so much energy into fighting disorder. Our job is essentially to suppress chaos. We make beds. We pick up trash. We pick up clothes. We wash clothes. We fold clothes. We put away clothes … theoretically. (I never quite make it past the folding stage, but you get the point.) Then, we go to bed and wake up and do it all again.

In pushing back against entropy, we are essentially fighting a law of the universe. It's either us or the universe, and my money is on the universe. And when you have small children, the chaos of entropy is just so obvious.

Every night, I go to bed after returning my home to some semblance of order. The dishes are done. The floor is picked up. The counters are clear. Maybe there is some mysterious sticky substance on the floor under my two-year-old's chair, but at least it doesn't look like a tornado went through our house.

Within minutes of my children waking the next day, everything is destroyed. Toys everywhere, crumbs all over the kitchen floor, pillow cushions strewn about the living room. I'm not sure how it even happens. The havoc they can wreak in such a short amount of time is awe-inspiring, and with such small hands too! I don't believe in the Big Bang Theory, but if I did, I imagine it would look something like my house at nine o'clock in the morning.

I sweep my floor multiple times a day, yet somehow, it is still always dirty. I have two theories about this. The first theory has to do with the critically acclaimed Disney Channel original movie *Smart House.* If you grew up in the 90s or early 2000s, I know you know this movie. The Smart Floor in this Smart House had an amazing feature—it would actually self-clean, sucking up dirt and trash! I think my floor is like that, only in reverse. I sweep and sweep and then … I'm convinced that the floor spits dirt and crumbs back up. That's right: I think I have a Stupid Floor.

My second theory as to why my floor remains dirty despite my attempts to clean it is that that there are tiny, sneaky dirt gremlins living in my home. They tiptoe behind me while I sweep and gleefully sprinkle dirt and Cheerio dust where I have just swept, always staying barely out of sight.

Of course, the other distinct possibility is that my floor stays dirty simply because I have children who have little to no regard for cleanliness or table manners and who devour their food like the Cookie Monster devours cookies. Whatever the case, it is impossible to keep the floor clean: my attempts to do so are clearly a hopeless battle against entropy.

So we fight entropy, but the universe will never let us win. Almost daily, I tell myself that it's futile and that I should just stop trying to have an orderly house, yet every day I still try. Some call that the definition of insanity. I call it motherhood.

The Quest for Peace in the Entropy

I am able to laugh about my daily chaos here in these paragraphs, but there are days, *many* days, when I find it anything but funny.

As an introvert, I thrive in peace and calm and quiet. My dream job is to be a librarian. Surrounded by books with no one to talk to? Sign me up. I *do* like people, contrary to some misconceptions of introverts. But people drain me, and I prefer to be alone more often than not. I dislike chaos and excessive stimulation. Too much of that with too little time alone and I will become agitated, exhausted, and short-tempered. So, naturally, I decided to become a stay-at-home mother of small children, a job that is clearly conducive to all of these predilections.

Some days the chaos of motherhood feels like too much, making me wonder if God chose the wrong person for this particular job. I can almost feel it sapping me of my strength and joy, robbing me of my peace. In fact, it often feels like peace is something that I am constantly chasing but never quite grasping.

After my third child was born, there were times when the chaos almost felt oppressive. I would be sitting in the middle of my mess of a house, sleep-deprived, nursing my son while also trying to manage a dispute my older two were having about whatever worthless McDonald's toy had suddenly become an object of great desire to them both. And at the back of my mind, there was always a long list of the things I needed to do. The remnants of lunch were still on the table. The laundry still sat in the dryer. There were doctor's appointments to schedule and errands to run.

I felt starved for peace and calm and quiet, but thought I had no hope of finding them. Even now as I try to write this, my two-year-old is sitting on my lap pressing all the wrong buttons, both literal and metaphorical. If I happen to unknowingly say something heretical here, I will blame it on him.

What does peace look like for a mother who lives

in chaos? How does she get it? And if she can somehow find it, how does she keep it?

As I struggled through those early days as a mom of three, a well-known verse kept running through my mind. I would be on my hands and knees, picking up Hot Wheels while my daughter sang loudly and off-key and my oldest said *Mommy* for the millionth time that day, hoping that if I rushed through dishes and got the baby down for his nap on time, that maybe, just maybe, I could sit down and breathe for a moment. I would be there, drowning in the chaos and cacophony, and the words, "Be still and know that I am God" would pop into my mind.

I bet you've seen that cross-stitched on a pillow somewhere. I'd always thought of this verse as a call to retreat to a quiet place. We simply need to find our *zen*, right? That is why I found this particular verse unhelpful. I couldn't go and find my *zen*. I hadn't seen my *zen* since 2014, before that harrowing ride home from the hospital with my firstborn baby. My obvious inability to be still was precisely the problem. How was I supposed to find peace when my day-to-day life was anything but peaceful?

I kept pushing the verse away, thinking it irrelevant, but it kept coming back. That still, small voice, gentle but persistent. *Be still and know ...* I finally picked up my Bible and searched for this very popular verse. And I discovered, maybe for the 100th time, that popular verses—so often pulled out of context—can only be rightly understood *in* context.

"Be still and know," comes from Psalm 46. Of course, I had read it before, but I don't think I had ever fully understood it. As it turns out, Psalm 46 is not a psalm about peace and quiet.

It's a psalm about chaos.

> God is our refuge and strength,
> a very present help in trouble.
> Therefore we will not fear though the earth gives way,
> though the mountains be moved into the heart of the sea,
> though its water roar and foam,
> though the mountains tremble at its swelling.
> (Psalm 46:1–3)

These first few verses of the psalm describe complete and utter chaos: mountains moving and trembling, the earth literally falling apart. While there may not be any actual mountains moving during days at home with little children, it can feel just as chaotic. If I had to rewrite these verses to describe motherhood, they would go something like this:

> God is our refuge and strength,
> a very present help in trouble.
> Therefore we will not fear though the toys scatter,
> though the laundry mountains tower,

though the children scream and cry,
though we sigh and grow weary of our tasks.

Why will we not fear? Because God is our help—our very present help—our refuge and strength. And where is our help? Not outside of trouble and chaos, but *in* it.

There is a River

I often feel that peace is something I am trying and failing to *achieve*. If only I could get the laundry done, then I could rest. If only I could finish cleaning the bathrooms, then I wouldn't feel so stressed. If only I could get the entire house perfectly in order and perfectly clean, then I'd finally feel at peace. I am constantly trying to *engineer* peace by eliminating the chaos. I try desperately to *create* peace externally so that I can feel peace internally.

Needless to say, these goals are pretty much unattainable. Trying to eliminate chaos and engineer peace in a home where small children live is like playing a never-ending game of Whac-A-Mole. Once you clean up one applesauce spill, a Go-Gurt and a smushed banana rise up to take its place. It's exhausting and ends up creating the opposite of what I want to achieve: rather than feeling peace inside, the never-ending chaos in my house and my futile attempts to get rid of it end up creating chaos in my heart. Psalm 46 speaks to this as well:

> There is a river whose streams make glad the city of God,
> the holy habitation of the Most High.
> God is in the midst of her; she shall not be moved;
> God will help her when morning dawns.
> The nations rage, the kingdoms totter;
> he utters his voice, the earth melts.
> The LORD of hosts is with us;
> the God of Jacob is our fortress. (Psalm 46:4–6)

What makes glad the city of God? What gives her peace and joy when everything around her is falling apart? Streams. Where do these streams come from? A river. A river with a single Divine source, spreading out in an array of streams to carry life and hope and renewal. A river that continues to flow even when war threatens all around. The psalm goes on to say that the Lord alone rules the nations that wage such war (verses 8–9). And that is when He tells us to be still and know Him (verse 10).

The call to be still and know is different from what the cross-stitched pillows might have us think, then. It's not a call to *create* perfect, external peace. It's not a call to *escape* chaos and find quiet. It's a call to find peace within the chaos. It's a call to have a quiet soul in a loud world. The secret to having peace in motherhood is not eliminating chaos. We could never do that anyway. Our best efforts only last about ten minutes. We cannot draw peace from the outside in but must radiate it from the inside out. The entropy of motherhood is not going anywhere. And the more children we have, the more it multiplies. We must stop chasing a peace that can be destroyed by chaos. We need a peace that is impervious to chaos, flowing from a single, everlasting source.

Paul hinted at the source of this amazing peace in his letter to the Philippians:

> I have learned in whatever situation I am to be content. I know how to be brought low, and I know how to abound. In any and every circumstance, I have learned the secret of facing plenty and hunger, abundance and need. I can do all things through Him who strengthens me. (Philippians 4:11–13)

What did Paul mean here? Was this some kind of self-empowerment speech, as many think? No. He was saying he had found a peace and contentment that existed independently of external circumstances—a joy that thrived in struggle.

Our souls hunger for this kind of lasting peace—a supernatural peace that only God can give. Christ, who did not run from our chaos but who stepped down into it, brought this peace into our midst—our crazy, messy midst. Now, the Lord of hosts is with us. *He* is our river. If we draw from His streams, He will make us glad. He will be our very present help.

And someday … someday, it won't be this way.

Someday, we'll have a clean, quiet house that only whispers the memories of messier, crazier times. There will be no sticky substance under the table or Cheerios in our sheets (I hope). Someday, we'll have all the alone time we want and an abundance of personal space. There will be no one grabbing our legs or squirming their way into our laps while we're trying to cram our lunch into our faces.

So for today, kiss your little electrons and let them hover as you soak your soul in the peace of God. He will be with us in the chaos, and He will help us when morning dawns.

Reflection Questions

1) What aspects of the chaos of motherhood bring you the most inward chaos and unrest? The endlessly dirty floor? Hearing *Mom!* for the 87th time in one morning? Why do those things seem especially challenging for you?

2) Is there a relationship between the quest for self-made identity we considered in chapter 6 and the quest for self-made peace? How do you see these desires at work in your own heart?

3) Think of moments in your day when the chaos tends to feel overwhelming. Maybe it's getting out the door for preschool, or the bedtime circus. Think of specific ways in which you can foster the peace of God in that

chaos. Choose a verse to speak to yourself, or post reminders to pray before you go into that situation.

8

Philosophy

The Endless Why of Toddlers and the Great Why of Motherhood

It is finally time for my favorite subject: philosophy. In philosophy, you spend a lot of time talking about something called *metaphysics*. If you don't really know what *metaphysics* means, that's okay. I have a degree in philosophy, and I still hardly know what it means. It's the kind of word that you hear defined, and then five minutes later, you forget the definition entirely. It's hard to remember because … well, it's so metaphysical.

Metaphysics is the branch of philosophy that deals with abstract concepts such as being, knowing, substance, cause, identity, time, and space. It describes what happens "beyond" the physical. Essentially, it is the study of being or existence.

As a student of metaphysics, I spent a lot of my time in classrooms discussing what it meant to say that our chairs existed and asking how we knew that they did. Maybe they didn't exist. Maybe *we* didn't exist. Maybe we are all brains in vats, and this world we experience is some kind of simulation. Yes, this is what enlightened, intellectual people talked about, and I paid good money for it when I probably could have just watched *The Matrix*.

As it turns out, though, small children are just as enlightened and intellectual as the most noble philosophers. This happens around two years of age when your children start asking really deep metaphysical questions. This is when they begin wanting to know *why*. About everything.

They will want to know why you are eating. Don't think that the superficial answer, "Because I'm hungry," will satisfy their voracious appetite for knowledge. They will want to know *why* you are hungry.

"Because I need to eat," you will tell them.

"But why?" they will demand.

"Because bodies need food."

"But why?"

"Because that's how God made bodies."

"But WHY?"

And then *you* will begin to wonder why God made bodies that way. *Why did God make anything the way that He made it? Why did He make anything at all? Why are we here? Why is there something rather than nothing?*

Before you know it, your children will have

turned your simple turkey and cheese sandwich into a deep, metaphysical quandary. They will do this about everything *ad nauseum*. Why is this a ball? Why are these your clothes? Why are you going to the bathroom? Why is my bow pink? What's more, they will start insisting that your answers to their questions are wrong. They will tell you that their bow is not pink. It's purple. (Can you say *postmodernism*?) Clearly, they know more than you do. The years you've got on them mean nothing.

Thus, you will find yourself in the most ridiculous discussions with your children. And at the end of it all, when they've worn you down with their endless questions, you will not be sure if they've dragged you down to their intellectual level, or if their level is actually so far above yours that you just can't hang. In any case, you're not sure why a ball is a ball other than it just *is*, but you sure don't have time to think too hard about it.

On the surface, it doesn't seem like small children and the stern-faced philosophers of old paintings would have much in common, but I bet your two-year-old would have some pretty great conversations with Hume and Descartes. "I'm two; therefore, I ask *why*?" could be the catchphrase of toddlers everywhere. So if you haven't brushed up on your metaphysics, you'd better get going. Soon, your budding philosopher will want to know things like why water is wet. Be ready to have multiple variants of the same answer because one will never be enough. As I learned while studying secular philosophy, their goal is not really to find answers but to find more questions. Children have an endless supply of those.

The "Why" of Motherhood

While we may be pulling our hair out, trying to deal with our children's apparently endless *why* questions, we may start asking a few questions of our own. *Why am I here? Why is motherhood so hard? Why is motherhood important?* Is *it important?* I found myself asking these very questions on a walk a few years ago.

"I think what this piece needs most is a vision for the glories of the day-in/day-out mothering that will capture the attention of other stay-at-home-moms." I had pitched an essay to a Christian website, and this is what the editor wrote back. I chewed on the words as I walked, weary from the day-in/day-out mothering to which he referred.

That particular day had been rough. The kids had covered themselves in dirt after a bath. My toddler had scribbled on a new white table and then thrown not only a toothbrush but also a ball and a rubber ducky in the toilet. I'd done what felt like five billion loads of laundry. And there had been lots of general whining and butt-wiping per usual.

A vision for the glories of motherhood? What was it? I wondered. The words *glories* and *motherhood* didn't seem to belong in the same sentence. There didn't seem to be anything obviously glorious about the stench of diapers or the endless laundry. I'd had a vision once for the beautiful call to raise my children according to God's Word, but ... I seemed to have lost it somewhere along the way between the newborn cuddles and the exhausting debates over having cake for breakfast with my newborn-turned-toddler. Hanging onto that vision felt like hanging onto sand. That's the trouble with motherhood: you can get so immersed *in* it that you lose the perspective you need to get *through* it.

That's why we should now take a little page out of the toddler handbook and talk about the *why* of motherhood. Because there must be a *why*. If there's not, none of what we do really makes any sense at all. We mothers are clearly not in it for the money or the great hours or the awesome things it does for our bodies. If this was an actual job, it would be the worst job ever. No pay. No bonus for good work. No time off. Oh, and you have to wipe your boss's butt. I'm calling H.R.

So ... why? Why did we have children? Why not get a puppy and travel the world instead? If you've never pondered this question and articulated an answer to it, it is important that you do. In philosophy, we call this *teleology*. For the Ancient Greek philosopher Aristotle, understanding the *telos* of something, or its end or purpose, was imperative to understanding the thing itself.

Motherhood without a *telos* is like a ship with no destination, a race with no finish line.

One of the best lines from arguably the best movie of all time, *It's a Wonderful Life,* comes when desperate, discouraged, downtrodden George Bailey grumbles, "Why do we have to have all these kids?" He'd wanted a different life, and he'd forgotten why and how he'd ended up with the life he had. At some point, we're all going to ask ourselves the same question. This job is going to get hard, just like it did for George, and we're going to need a renewed vision—a fresh view of our *telos.*

Called to Glory

As I walked that day and tried to recall why I had decided to have all these kids, I thought back to the spring of my senior year of college. On the brink of embarking upon my own journey into adulthood, my future was undecided. It was simultaneously terrifying and thrilling. As a philosophy major, my path was narrower than I had realized. I know it might be surprising, but there aren't many listings for philosophers on Indeed.com. Not many employers seemed impressed with my thorough understanding of Aristotle's Four

Causes. Still, I was sure God was going to take me on some grand and glorious adventure.

I knew the big-picture answer of my purpose on earth: to glorify God and enjoy him forever. The problem was that while I did want to live for God's glory, my understanding of how to do that was skewed.

Glory sounds like such a grand term. It evokes images of battlefield sacrifices or marathon finishes. I thought that meant I had to do spectacular things for God. But years later, I haven't. In fact, my life often feels anything but spectacular.

The early days of motherhood were certainly hard and sometimes overwhelming, but it was also occasionally boring. I loved being home with my son and watching him grow and change, but I also sometimes struggled with the fact that my world had become so small. Most of my days were passed inside the same four walls. Most of my days consisted of doing the same common tasks over and over. Most of my days involved an abundance of poop. After years of being involved in many activities, going to college, and feeling like my life was full of possibility, I struggled a little with the fact that my life was so … ordinary. It felt almost like an anti-climax. Yet it was during that time that God began to reshape my vision of what it meant to glorify Him.

I remember going to a party around that time to celebrate my grandparents' sixtieth wedding anniversary.

In one sense, their lives had been unremarkable. Jon and Dorothy were childhood sweethearts who became husband and wife. They had stayed faithful to each other for sixty years. They lived most of their lives in the state they grew up in. My grandfather worked one job for most of his career. They had two children whom they did their best to raise. My grandmother was often at the sink doing dishes or cooking a meal for a family dinner. And those ordinary things made their lives extraordinary. Those very things led to a loving family of seven grandchildren and sixteen (at the moment) great-grandchildren—a legacy that will last far beyond Jon and Dorothy. Their everyday faithfulness became the firm foundation on which I and many others now stand.

As I considered this legacy at my grandparents' anniversary party, I began to see that glorifying God might be less about doing adventurous and remarkable things and more about being faithful in the humble and ordinary seasons of life that not many see. Now as a mom, I know the truth that doing small, ordinary things for God is, in some ways, much harder than trying to do big, "important" things for God.

This is not to say that I still don't sometimes struggle with the humdrum cadences of life as a mother. Usually, the only adventurous or remarkable thing I manage to do on any given day is wrestle my toddler into a diaper or maybe leave the house. The car seat struggle is real, folks. On a really good day, maybe I vacuum and mop the entire house.

There can be an almost mind-numbing regularity and repetitiveness to my days. Make meals, clean up, change diapers, put away toys, and then wake up and do it all again. I can grow tired of the monotony—the sameness of my tasks, the dishes I've washed countless times, the laundry I'm sure I *just* folded, that Stupid Floor that never seems to stay clean.

Maybe like me, you sometimes wonder, *What is the point of it all?*

Called to Die

The truth is, motherhood is not a hobby or a means to personal happiness or simply what you do because society tells you to. Motherhood is a calling, and it's not like how I feel called to take more naps or to go on more Instagram-worthy vacations. *Calling* is a word that sounds grandiose and glamorous, but for the Christian, it carries a humbler meaning. Because each of us is *called* to die.

Jesus told his disciples before He was crucified, "The hour has come for the Son of Man to be glorified" (John 12:23). I wonder if the disciples were expecting trumpeters to come and usher Jesus to His throne. But what comes next is *not* what any of us would expect. It doesn't sound glorious at all: "Truly, truly, I say to you, unless a grain of wheat falls into the earth and dies, it remains alone; but if it dies, it bears much fruit" (John 12:24).

Jesus was telling his disciples a mysterious truth—*the* mysterious truth. Death is the gateway to life. Sacrifice is the path to glory, and it is the path He cleared for us to follow.

The trouble is that none of us want to die. We want the glory without the death, the reward without the sacrifice. None of us wants to be that grain that falls to the ground, forgotten and trampled amidst the dirt. We want to be the full and golden head of wheat, waving in the wind.

Jesus didn't want to die either. He pleaded for the cup to pass from Him, yet He went to the cross willingly anyway. Why? Scripture tells us that it was "for the joy that was set before Him" (Hebrews 12:2). Jesus had a vision that he clung to—a *telos*. He kept in view the purpose, or the *why*, of His suffering and sacrifice. He knew that the grain that falls to the ground and dies today will reap a bountiful harvest in years to come.

Called to Change the World

Remember the walk I took after that editor recommended that I write about the glories in the daily work of motherhood? Here is what I thought about on that walk. I thought about how I had decided to give myself to the calling of motherhood because God was changing my vision of what it meant to glorify

Him. I believed that if I wanted to "change the world" and have an impact for God's kingdom—to do something truly great—then I would pour my life not into chasing my own success or acclaim but into raising up the next generation to be lights in this dark world. If I really wanted to make something of myself, I would multiply—not only physically, but spiritually.

This is the calling of motherhood, to fall to the ground and die *that we might bear much fruit*. This is the glorious vision under all the monotony of dishes and the nitty-gritty ritual of bedtime routines. It's a vision that is both smaller and bigger than what we would choose for ourselves. It's a vision that shrinks our view of ourselves but expands our view of God and eternity.

As we move through the day-to-day motions of diapers and laundry and dishes, we meet both our curse and our redemption, for we are caught somewhere between the *already* and the *not yet*. Through sin, all things have been subjected to entropy and futility, but through Christ, all things are being restored (Romans 8:18–21). To live truly spiritual, God-glorifying lives, we must every day reclaim as holy what the fall made accursed, including the toil of everyday labor and the painful, wearying work of child-bearing and child-rearing. As we work in or out of the home, we are working alongside Christ to restore what has been broken. Nothing in our lives is merely secular or pointless now. Nothing is too small or too trivial to do without joy and purpose. All ground on which we tread is holy ground, and all work to which we put our hands is holy work.

The difficulty is that motherhood doesn't always feel holy, and it certainly doesn't look holy. It looks crude and unrefined and messy. It looks like spilled applesauce and feels like jelly-covered hands.

What I've learned and continue to relearn is that importance cannot be measured in audience members or in applause or even in difficulty. The greatest of tasks can be cloaked in the humble and ordinary. Purpose is not always tangible, and it is often delayed in fulfillment. The one who sows the seed waters the earth long before she sees any reason to do so, and even then, it is many years before the seed becomes a great tree. In the same way, the fruits of our labor as mothers are long in coming. Before us, we find little ones who are so helpless, so needy, so self-focused that it can be hard to imagine them as anything else.

On days when motherhood is hard, I try to picture my sons and daughter as I hope they will someday be: men and women who, like trees planted by streams of water (Jeremiah 17:7–8), put their confidence in Jesus. I envision my sons as men mature in the faith, "like plants full grown," and my daughter as a woman strong in the faith, like a pillar "cut for the structure of a palace" (Psalm 144:12).

I am only one ordinary person. What can I give this world? To answer this question, I must first ask what the world needs. It needs men and women who look like Jesus, whose lives are anchored in His word. That's my vision. That's what I hope to give the world. That's why I get up every day (and often several times throughout the night) to do this job that no one in their right mind would apply for. It's for His glory and it's for their good.

If we can hang onto *that* vision, we will remember that we are laboring in our homes so that they are places *where our children may meet Jesus*. We are persevering in our often monotonous work so that we might create places of peace, of love, of grace—fertile ground for the renewal of the precious souls whom God has entrusted to us. This is our *telos.* This is our great, glorious gospel-task, which manifests itself in such small and humble ways.

So, weary Momma, hold tightly to your *why*. Persevere in the monotony, and don't waste it. Show your kids how God imbues our mundane lives with meaning. Teach them that bringing order to a room reflects the Creator, how cooking a meal shows love, and how enjoying it magnifies God's goodness. Show your children ordinary faithfulness. As you do, you will point them to Jesus.

If you find yourself asking *why*, I hope you remember this vision. By God's grace, there is a day coming when your children will be like that tree planted by the stream that is Christ, bearing much fruit and offering shade to the weary. Then they will know what we are now learning: the most important things in life are often what make us the least important. The greatest life is the life given away.

Reflection Questions

1) Who do you know who has modeled "ordinary faithfulness"? What has been the fruit? How does the gospel free us to be content with living such ordinary lives?

2) Jesus showed us that the path to glory and joy is through death to self, yet it is hard and even unnatural to want that. Think of a time when you have practiced death to self. What fruit did you bear in that season? How did your faith—the assurance of things hoped for, but not seen—enable you to follow that path?

3) Consider your *telos*. If motherhood is a marathon, what is the finish line? What has God called you to as a mother? What does faithfulness look like in your particular home with your particular children—in the sphere God has given you? Take the answers to these questions and write a vision statement for your motherhood. Consider adding a theme verse and put it somewhere where you will be reminded of it regularly.

Graduation Day

As We Go Forth

So, here we are at the end of our lessons. We've covered a lot of ground in our "mom degree." We've talked about the poop and the purpose, the grime and the glory. I hope you have laughed *and* have been encouraged to press on in the hardest, messiest, most glorious job in the world.

I guess you could call this our graduation ceremony. Pretend *Pomp and Circumstance* is playing in the background. *Buuuum bum bum buum buuuum bum*.... This ceremony is definitely light on the pomp, though. Imagine me handing you a diploma scribbled with crayon and framed with a few dried macaroni noodles. You've made it! You're graduating. Except ... I'm not sure you ever *really* graduate when it comes to this job, never really get to leave the basics behind.

The eighteenth-century writer Samuel Johnson once wrote that people need reminding more than instructing, and I find that rings true. Someday, I'm sure you won't need the formula for Hangry, and toddler physics will be a thing of the past, but I don't think you'll ever "move on" from needing to be reminded of the truths we've discussed in this book. It has now been a few years since I started writing it, and I know I haven't outgrown them yet. In fact, there are many times when I catch myself still trying to find my identity in motherhood or living out of my own strength and I think, *You need to go back and listen to your own words, Emily.* You see … no matter how much we grow, we never outgrow our need for the gospel.

And so, even as I send you off, I hope you will come back and get reminders when you need them. Remember that though this job often feels humanly impossible, "He who calls you is faithful; He will surely do it" (1 Thessalonians 5:24). Remember that though the days are often long and the work humble, your calling is great.

Behind every great man or woman of the faith was a faithful mother who changed their diapers. Someone fed Charles Spurgeon pureed peas. Somebody taught Elisabeth Elliot her ABCs. Even Jesus had to grasp tightly to Mary's hand before He could walk on His own. Every believer stands on a foundation laid by someone else. Every warrior for the kingdom first heard the gospel from someone else. Our children will first hear it from us. What a privilege. What a vision. Grab it and run.

Author

Emily Schuch is an Oklahoma native who studied philosophy at the University of Oklahoma. She blogs at IlluminatingTruth.org and her writing has appeared at DesiringGod.org. She and her husband live in Frisco, Texas, where she cares for their six children.

Acknowledgements

Thank you to all those at Cruciform Press for making this book a reality and helping me reach other moms in the trenches.

Thank you to my amazing editor Elizabeth Berget for poring over every word of this book with me and giving me her perspective as a mother. Countless hours and email exchanges brought it from a half-baked manuscript to a far more complete and cohesive version of itself.

And, lastly, thank you to my husband, Stephen, who has always encouraged me in my writing and believed I had this book in me. He was my sounding board throughout this entire process, many times talking me off the cliff of self-doubt and urging me to press on and trust the Lord.

JESSALYN HUTTO

Comfort in Pregnancy Loss

TIM CHALLIES

Great Men and their Godly Moms

MCPHAIL, MENCHINGER

JERRY BRIDGES

Our Identity in Christ

PIPER, WOLGEMUTH, 11 MORE

Thirty Marriage Devitoonals

JONATHAN HOLMES

Inductive Bible Studies for Women from Keri Folmar

PHILIPPIANS

10 Weeks

EPHESIANS

10 Weeks

JAMES

GOSPEL OF MARK, VOL. 1

Son of God

11 Weeks

GOSPEL OF MARK, VOL. 2

11 Weeks

TITUS

Printed in the USA
CPSIA information can be obtained
at www.ICGtesting.com
CBHW051119210424
7298CB00014B/1194